STUDY GU

HOW TO WALK IN THE
Supernatural
POWER
of GOD

GUILLERMO MALDONADO

WHITAKER
HOUSE

How to Walk in the Supernatural Power of God Study Guide

Guillermo Maldonado
13651 S.W. 143rd Ct., #101
Miami, FL 33186
www.ERJPub.org

ISBN: 978-1-60374-326-6
Printed in the United States of America
© 2011 by Guillermo Maldonado

Whitaker House
1030 Hunt Valley Circle
New Kensington, PA 15068
www.whitakerhouse.com

2 3 4 5 6 7 8 9 10 11 🕮 18 17 16 15 14 13 12 11

STUDY GUIDE

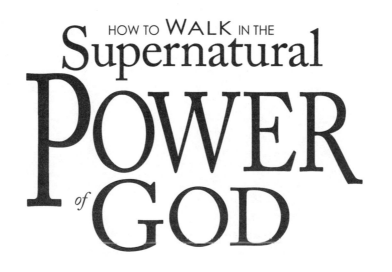

Contents

1

The Revelation of a Supernatural God

Man has tried to know his Creator through intellectual means, but this has proven impossible because God can be known only through revelation. In fact, He has always desired for us to know Him intimately and to experience His attributes, strengths, and virtues. This is why He sent us His Holy Spirit. No person has the mental ability to describe the infinite or the eternal. However, I will try to present a basic and uncomplicated description that will help you to understand Him in human terms.

Who Is God?

God is a _spiritual_ [1], _eternal_ [2], and immutable being with supernatural attributes and abilities. He dwells in the dimension of eternity—the spiritual realm—and manifests in visible form in the natural dimension.

Thus says the High and Lofty One who inhabits eternity. (Isaiah 57:15)

What is Revelation?

In Greek, "revelation" is the word *apokalypsis* which means "laying bare, making naked… a _disclosure_ [3] of truth, instruction concerning things before unknown." This expression is used, mostly, to express something that exists in the spiritual realm, and it expresses "spiritual perception." Revelation means to suddenly understand something without research or natural means of learning.

Revelation

Revelation is the knowledge of God revealed to our spirits, and it is received by spiritually seeing, hearing, and perceiving. This process is referred to as "spiritual perception." Revelation allows you to _suddenly_ [4] understand something without the aid of the natural senses.

Flesh and blood has not revealed this to you, but My Father who is in heaven. (Matthew 16:17)

To receive revelation from God is to see as He sees, to hear as He hears, and to perceive as He perceives.

Revelation includes knowing things you should not know, seeing things that have yet to occur, and *perceiving* (5) things without prior knowledge. It is the mind of God revealed so that mankind can exercise dominion over time, space, and matter.

In the absence of progressive divine revelation, people tend to turn to formal, *natural* (6) intellectual education, much of which serves to discredit faith. Intellectual knowledge has its rightful place in society, but it is a poor substitute for spiritual knowledge.

Who Is the Source of Revealed Knowledge?

The Source of all revelation is the *Holy Spirit* (7). He is the only channel that gives us access to God's revealed wisdom or knowledge. The Holy Spirit hears what is said in heaven and repeats it to men and women on earth. We cannot know God without the help of the Holy Spirit.

How Did the Apostle Paul Handle Natural Knowledge?

However, we speak wisdom among those who are mature, yet not the wisdom of this age, nor of the rulers of this age, who are coming to nothing. But we speak the wisdom of God in a mystery, the hidden wisdom which God ordained before the ages for our glory.

(1 Corinthians 2:6–7)

Philosophy is a science based on a *love* (8) of *wisdom* (9) that is obtained from the natural environment. Paul, upon his return to the church in Corinth, he emphatically expressed that he had returned in God's power and not in human wisdom. Paul understood that human wisdom and philosophy were *incapable* (10) of producing the supernatural power required to preach the gospel or to manifest God's power.

God's Wisdom

The mystery which has been hidden from ages and from generations, but now has been revealed to His saints. To them God willed to make known what are the riches of the glory of this mystery among the Gentiles: which is Christ in you, the hope of glory.

(Colossians 1:26, 27)

The wisdom of our Lord Jesus Christ is to share His secrets through the cross.

Eye has not seen, nor ear heard, nor have entered into the heart of man the things which God has prepared for those who love Him. (1 Corinthians 2:9)

The natural senses alone cannot perceive the revealed wisdom or knowledge of God.

But God has revealed them to us through His Spirit. For the Spirit searches all things, yes, the deep things of God. For what man knows the things of a man except the spirit of the man which is in him? Even so no one knows the things of God except the Spirit of God.

(1 Corinthians 2:10–11)

Four Truths That Can Be Known Only Through Revelation:

- The nature of *God* [11]
- The nature of *man* [12]
- The origin of man
- The origin of life

These truths cannot be fully discovered through scientific, natural, psychological, psychiatric, or philosophical means. Scientists and avid students seek to use only mental processes and the systematic collection of information acquired through the natural senses. Within such limitations, they have no choice but to deny God because their workable knowledge does not allow them to accept Him. Sensory knowledge cannot explain the origin of creation or the beginning of matter, and it lacks valid answers to the great "whys" of humanity. Scientists have developed diverse theories on the *origin* [13] of life and the nature of God. They have written countless volumes on the subject, all derived from the same restrictive sources. Formal education has contributed to the destruction of the *faith* [14] of millions of young people who were raised and trained to recognize and accept only that which they can see, feel, decipher, and explain with their physical senses and intellect.

The only way to know God and to relate to His supernatural
and invisible realm is by faith.

God is always the One who chooses to reveal Himself to us; thus, we must *depend* [15] solely on Him. If God had not chosen to reveal Himself, we never would have known Him.

God's Revelation Depends On:

- God's *time* [16]
- God's *will* [17]

God said that in the last days, *knowledge* [18] would increase (see Daniel 12:3–4) because it is His will to fill the earth with His glory. (See Numbers 14:21.) I believe that we are living in those last days, days in which the manifestation of His glory will be evident everywhere.

Your faith will be strongest in the area in which you have the greatest *revealed* [19] knowledge from God. Likewise, your faith will be weakest where you lack revelation or have little of it.

The enemy establishes a stronghold where God's knowledge
and revelation do not exist.

What Are the Two Realms That Exist?

- The *natural* [20] realm
- The *supernatural* [21] realm

What is the natural realm? It is the dimension that is subject to the ___*time*___ (22), space, and matter, a dimension that can be accessed only through the physical senses.

What is the supernatural realm? It is the dimension that operates ___*above*___ (23) natural laws. It is the spiritual realm—permanent, invisible, and eternal—located outside of time. It exercises dominion over the natural realm. The spiritual realm can be accessed only by faith.

We do not look at the things which are seen, but at the things which are not seen. For the things which are seen are temporary, but the things which are not seen are eternal.

(2 Corinthians 4:18)

What is a miracle?

I define a *miracle* as "the supernatural ___*intervention*___ (24) of God that interrupts the normal course of the natural life." When God stops the clock of time and puts His finger on a situation, a miracle takes place. When He removes His finger, natural time resumes once again. He is a God of miracles. And we see this in the following examples from Scripture.

God Stops the Sun

Then Joshua...said in the sight of Israel: "Sun, stand still over Gibeon; and Moon, in the Valley of Aijalon." So the sun stood still, and the moon stopped, till the people had revenge upon their enemies.   (Joshua 10:12–13)

According to discoveries in astronomy, we now know that the earth orbits the sun, not the other way around. When Joshua gave the order, therefore, it was actually the earth that stood still, not the sun. In addition to orbiting the sun, the earth also rotates on its axis, making a complete turn every twenty-four hours at a speed close to one thousand miles per hour. This rotation is what produces night and day, sunrise and sunset. With this in mind, why did Joshua order the sun to stop if it is the earth that is in orbit? Joshua was simply speaking from his point of view. The most incredible aspect of this miracle is that the earth actually did ___*stand still*___ (25)! It stopped rotating without being destroyed. We cannot limit God. He is supernatural and all-powerful. He has complete and total dominion over nature.

In the Old Testament, God showed Himself to be a supernatural God of miracles,

- At the Tower of Babel, He divided the people by giving them new languages (see Genesis 11:5–8);

- At Sodom and Gomorrah when God destroyed entire cities with fire from heaven (see Genesis 19:24–25.);

- God saved Moses from Pharaoh's plot to kill Israel's firstborn sons (see Exodus 12);

- In the desert, God spoke to Moses from a bush that burned without being consumed (see Exodus 3);

- In Pharaoh's palace, God turned Aaron's rod into a serpent (see Exodus 7:10–12), turned the Nile River into blood (see Exodus 7:14–24), and caused plagues of frogs, lice, flies, boils, and locusts (see Exodus 7–10);

- God parted the Red Sea and delivered Israel out of Egypt and slavery (see Exodus 13:17– 14:29);

- In the wilderness, God caused manna to descend from heaven every day (see Exodus 16:1–24), sent quail for them to eat (see Numbers 11:31–32), and drew water from a rock (see Exodus 17:6);

- He caused earthquakes to defeat and drive off the Philistines (see 1 Samuel 14:15);

- He destroyed the walls of Jericho (see Joshua 6);

- He caused an axe to float on water (see 2 Kings 6:6);

- He gave Samson the strength to kill lions and tear down the columns of the Philistines (see Judges 16:21–30);

- He gave Abraham and his sterile wife, Sarah, a son in their old age (see Genesis 21:1–3);

- He enabled a young shepherd named David to kill a giant named Goliath with only a sling and a stone (see 1 Samuel 17);

- He fed the widow of Zarephath with the multiplication of oil (see 1 Kings 17:8–15);

- He caused a donkey to speak (see Numbers 22–24);

- He consumed Elijah's sacrifice on Mount Carmel (see 1 Kings 18:16–46);

- He commanded rain to fall after a drought (see 1 Kings 18:16–46);

- He healed Naaman through His prophet (see 2 Kings 5:1–19);

- He raised Elisha's bones from the dead (2 Kings 13:14, 20–21);

- He kept Shadrach, Meshach, and Abed-Nego safe and unharmed in a fiery furnace (see Daniel 3);

- He kept Daniel safe when the king placed him in a lions' den (see Daniel 6:10–23);

- He preserved the life of Jonah in the belly of a whale (see Jonah 1–2).

And these are but a few examples.

We also see a miracle when God sent His only Son, Jesus, to reveal the heavenly Father as a supernatural God, and when His Son performed spectacular miracles, such as when He:

- Turned water into wine (see John 2:1–11);

- Healed the ten lepers, a centurion's servant, a paralytic, Peter's mother-in-law, and a deaf-mute (see, for example, Luke 17:11–19; Matthew 8:5–13; Luke 5:17–26; Mark 1:29–39; Mark 7:31–37);

- Straightened the back of the woman who had been bent for many years (see Luke 13:10– 17);

- Healed the blind beggar by the pool (see Mark 10:46–52);

- Restored the sight to one who was blind from birth (see John 9:1–25);

- Raised the son of the widow of Nain from the dead (see Luke 7:11–17);

- Delivered the daughter of the Syro-Phoenician woman (see Mark 7:24–30);

- Raised Lazarus three days after his death (see John 11:1–27);

- Multiplied the bread and the fish and fed five thousand people (see Mark 6:30–44);

- Walked on water (see Matthew 14:22–33);

- Pulled money from the mouth of a fish (see Matthew 17:24–27);

- Cursed the fig tree causing it to dry up (see Matthew 21:18–21),

- And delivered a demon-possessed man (see Mark 5:1–20).

Most of all, we see it when Jesus surrendered to the cross, descended into hell, took the keys of death from Satan, and was raised from the dead before ascending to heaven and sending us His Holy Spirit. In addition, we see it in the miracles that took place in the early church. And we continue to marvel at the miracles, signs, and wonders God performs in the church today.

The Two Sources of Supernatural Power

- *God* (26)

- *Satan* (27)

Any supernatural power that does not come from God is from Satan. Therefore, we must be *alert* (28) to avoid being *deceived* (29).

Then God blessed them, and God said to them, "Be fruitful and multiply; fill the earth and subdue it." (Genesis 1:28)

Man was created with God's supernatural power to exercise dominion and *lordship* (30) on the earth. He was not created to trust solely in his natural abilities, mind, reasoning, or any other source of sensorial knowledge offered by the world. Man was created to walk in the supernatural power of God.

The Supernatural God Revealed Himself Through Jesus

And Peter answered [Jesus] and said, "Lord, if it is You, command me to come to You on the water." So [Jesus] said, "Come." And when Peter had come down out of the boat, he walked on the water to go to Jesus. (Matthew 14:28–29)

Walking on water is one of Jesus' most awesome miracles. When Peter saw Him, he said he wanted to do the same thing and Jesus answered, *"Come."* As soon as Peter started to walk on the water, however, he felt the strong wind and focused on the storm, took his *eyes* (31) off of Jesus, and began to sink. Notice that Jesus did not rebuke Peter for wanting to walk on water, too. On the contrary, Jesus encouraged Peter to do it. Why did Peter want to walk on water? What was his motive? Peter left the safety of the boat because he was prompted by the instinctual need for *supernatural* (32) power that resides in man, the desire to cross over the line from the natural into the supernatural. Unfortunately, that same instinctual need has led many men away from God and toward more destructive supernatural options, such as magic, witchcraft, diabolical games, false religions, satanic sects, idolatry, and much more.

Today, we will notice that some rely solely on their natural abilities, trusting only in science, technology, mathematics, philosophy, logic, and other branches of human intellect and *understanding* (33). Others opt for witchcraft or other ungodly supernatural powers. Many fail to realize that their choices lead to idolatry and dissatisfaction. For this reason, God is raising a new generation with the audacity to leave the boat and walk on the water. This new generation wants more because God has placed that desire within them.

Today's Generation

When this generation goes to church looking for God's supernatural power, most do not find it because many churches preach a Jesus who is *dead* [34] and historic—a man from Sunday school stories. To these people, the powerful, supernatural, real, living, raised-from-the-dead Jesus remains a complete stranger. As a result, when people witness a miracle today, they are unable to believe it because they lack the *revelation* [35] of the true Christ. Due to this lack of power in the church, many young people have returned to the world in search of another source of power—that of the devil.

Most young adults have never witnessed or heard about God's supernatural power due to their unstable faith founded on human wisdom rather than on the revelation of Jesus. Today, many seek "supernatural" power by other means, including drugs, alcohol, divination, and witchcraft. Their desire for power is good, but the way they are trying to satisfy this desire is evil. Therefore, they become easy targets for the devil, who seeks to destroy them.

Enemies of the Supernatural God

1. *Ignorance* [36]

Therefore my people have gone into captivity, because they have no knowledge.

(Isaiah 5:13)

When the people lack knowledge, they are held captive in their ignorance.

2. Bad *Theology* [37]

Theology is the study of God through the mind and reason. When we study God with improper motivation, or without inspiration, illumination, and revelation from the Holy Spirit, theology becomes carnal. We need theology, but only that which comes by revelation imparted by the Holy Spirit.

3. *Humanism* [38]

Humanism is the collection of philosophical ideas that elevate man to the highest position in terms of esteem.

4. The "Spirit of Jezebel," or Witchcraft

O foolish Galatians! Who has bewitched you that you should not obey the truth...?

(Galatians 3:1)

The apostle Paul used the word "bewitched," which means "to bring evil on one by feigning praise or an evil eye...to charm, to bewitch." In Paul's mind, witchcraft was blinding the people's understanding and keeping them from recognizing the redeeming work of Christ on the cross.

The door to witchcraft is rebellion, which consists of stirring up or subverting any authorities established by God. Rebellion replaces divine authority with an illegitimate one.

5. The Carnal Mind

I want to clarify that it is not bad to have an intelligent, brilliant mind, as long as that mind is submissive to the leading of the Holy Spirit. The apostle Paul was a brilliant man, yet he learned to trust the illumination of the Holy Spirit rather than the carnal mind.

By nature, the carnal mind is anti-God.

What Happened at the Beginning of Creation?

The fall of man occurred when Adam substituted the revelation of God for the carnal mind, or mental knowledge and *common sense* [39]. He disobeyed the command of God:

But of the tree of the knowledge of good and evil you shall not eat. (Genesis 2:17)

After Adam sinned, time, space, and matter became the foundation of his reality. Sin took from him the ability to see into the spiritual realm. Today, the carnal mind still determines our reality until we are born again. When we receive Jesus, we begin the process of renewing our minds with God's thoughts. Our reality is determined by the level of revelation we have from Him. God gave us faith to enable us to exit the natural realm in which we had fallen.

What Can Take Us Beyond the Natural Dimension?

- Revelation, or *revealed* [40] knowledge

- Faith

So then, those who are in the flesh cannot please God. (Romans 8:8)

We need to raise a generation of believers who are not afraid or skeptical of the supernatural.

Common sense and human reasoning can never produce a miracle.

The Church of Human Ability

The church today tends to operate on the basis of human abilities. If something doesn't fall within the scope of what is considered "normal," it is not to be *believed* [41]. Consequently, nothing supernatural ever happens. Why, then, do we even go to church? Would we go to our jobs if we didn't expect to be paid? Would we go to a restaurant if we didn't expect to eat? Why would we go to church if we don't expect to witness miracles or experience some supernatural event—a healing, a new song, a new sign, or a miracle? If none of these occurs in the church, something is not right.

Humanism has robbed us of this expectancy. Many leaders and ministers have become stagnant and irrelevant, failing to generate any change or affect an impact within their nations. The time has come to retake the path set by the early church and return once again to the revelation of the living Christ, raised, all-powerful, and supernatural.

Action Steps

- If you genuinely desire to know the supernatural God, ask the Holy Spirit to open your understanding and reveal His greatness, His majesty, His love, and His supernatural power.

- Receive this prayer: Right now, I declare by faith that your eyes, ears, and spiritual senses will be opened to receive a supernatural experience with the living, real, supernatural Christ.

2

Substitutes for the Supernatural Power of God

What Is the Kingdom of God?

The kingdom of God is the invisible, divine government that is established on earth when the will of its King has been carried out completely. It is His administration influencing the earth, replacing its mundane operating system and order. The kingdom of God is the lordship and dominion on earth of King Jesus manifested in a visible form.

Jesus spoke of three divine realms:

*For Yours is the **kingdom** and the **power** and the **glory** forever.*

(Matthew 6:13, emphasis added)

The *"kingdom"* is the government of God; the *"power"* is the ability found in God; the *"glory"* is the presence of God.

The essence of Jesus' teaching is the kingdom, the power, and the glory.

In Acts 1, Jesus spent around forty days teaching His disciples about the kingdom. His goal was to prepare them for the day when they would receive the _power_ [(42)], an event that takes place in chapter 2 and is followed in chapter 3 by the manifestation of God's glory. Today, some ministries teach much about God's kingdom but with little demonstration of His power. In other ministries, the opposite occurs—there is a great manifestation of God's power, but little mention is made of the kingdom. In still other ministries, there is teaching on the glory but no manifestation of the power or God's kingdom. Jesus taught His disciples about the kingdom because He understood that to be effective witnesses in a hostile world, they would need the power.

What Generates the Revelation of the Kingdom in the Believers?

• **Structure**

The revelation of the kingdom produces within us a spirit that knows how to use God's _authority_ [(43)] and how to submit to it. Without this knowledge, such power may destroy people.

• **Order**

Order cannot be established in the absence of government and authority. Chaos and disorder can become dangerous when faced with the power of God.

• **Vision**

Without the kingdom's vision, power can become futile or _destructive_ [44].

• **Purpose**

Knowledge—or revelation—of the kingdom must come first in our lives. After revelation comes, power must have a purpose; otherwise, it can destroy.

What Is the Power of God?

The Greek word for "power" is *dynamis*. This word also means "powerful force, potency, or inherent power." *Dynamis* is the ability to perform miracles. It is the explosive, dynamic, and inherent power of God—His supernatural ability. When we speak of the reality of God, we cannot separate it from what exists in the natural. His power is intrinsically tied to the message of the gospel, and this is where the difference between Christianity and other religions, which cannot produce a supernatural experience, is rooted. In the book of Acts, the supernatural power of God is present in each of its twenty-eight chapters.

Religion is the result of not having an experience with God.

Substitutes for the Power of God

The spirit of witchcraft is in operation wherever you find carnal habits and legalistic practices.

The Galatians had started out in the Spirit: they were saved, were filled with the Spirit, and witnessed miracles, signs, and wonders. But _witchcraft_ [45] influenced them to follow rules, norms, and carnal ways, which caused them to lose sight of God's power.

The church today is in a similar situation. Let us recall that man is a spirit who has a soul and lives in a body. The soul has legitimate functions, but it cannot take the place of the spirit. When people begin to put their trust in their own abilities and strength, they move away from the spirit and toward the soul, which includes intellect and emotions. Then, a substitution takes place in which "religion" takes over for spiritual reality. Let us look at some of the most common substitutes.

• **Theology, lacking inspiration from the Holy Spirit, replaces revelation.**

Theology is man studying God with his human mind and _reasoning_ [46]. This is a proper way to study Him, but in order for it to be effective, man needs the revelation of the Holy Spirit. In other words, mankind needs to balance the knowledge he derives from studying God's Word with the knowledge he gets from Holy Spirit. This combination of the Spirit and the Word is what transforms our lives.

• **Intellectual education replaces character.**

Education occupies an important place in the life of an individual. Thus, it is important for young people to study, pursue educational degrees, and become excellent professionals. However, we must keep in mind that intellectual education does not build or shape their character; it only prepares them to carry out a job. The only thing that can shape character and transform the heart of man is the power of God.

It is very dangerous to train people intellectually without dealing with their character.

- **Psychology and psychiatry replace spiritual discernment.**

Psychology is part of the philosophy that studies the soul and the *mind* [47]. Psychiatry is the science that studies the psyche of the human mind and the illnesses connected to it. Psychologists and psychiatrists have the best intensions to help people, but they do not deal with the roots of their problems, which are spiritual. They deal only with the symptoms—the branches, which are superficial.

- **Man-made programs replace the leading of the Holy Spirit.**

The Bible teaches that in order for our works to prosper, God must take the initiative. (See, for example, Proverbs 16:3; 16:9 NIV) Unfortunately, many churches carry out their services according to their own agendas.

- **Eloquence replaces the demonstration of power.**

People run after personality-driven churches that are built on human *charisma* [48], talents, and gifts instead of on the name of Jesus.

- **Administrators replace apostles and prophets.**

Apostles and prophets bring the revelation and power that create breakthrough within the church. They are empowered by God with the anointing for spiritual warfare.

- **Reason, logic, and a carnal mind replace living by faith.**

When we handle divine situations with a carnal mind, we *limit* [49] God and lose hold of the supernatural. Faith gives us the ability to believe above human reason because it supersedes all reasoning.

- **Motivational preaching replaces the message of the cross.**

Motivational preaching is good because it inspires people, but when it is done without Jesus Christ as its central figure, it has no power to change hearts.

- **Rigid laws, norms, and regulations replace love.**

Many churches are more concerned with people keeping the *traditions* [50], norms, rules, and regulations of the council or denomination than offering the genuine love of Christ to the lost. Love is the only thing that can loosen God's power.

- **Entertainment replaces power.**

Many believers attend church in search of entertainment, and many leaders use entertainment as a means of keeping membership numbers high without fully establishing anyone in the power of God.

When we entertain people, we have lost the power.

• Human ability replaces God's grace.

Grace is the divine ability given by God for His people to become _everything_ [51] He has called us to be and to achieve that which we are unable to do in our own strength. Christ was the only perfect Man, and His life was a manifestation of God's supernatural power. He maintained a balance between His power and His character.

• Traditions replace the Word.

You…[make] the word of God of no effect through your tradition which you have handed down.

(Mark 7:13)

In some Christian circles, it is common to hear preaching that is based on traditions that have been passed down from generation to generation. The leaders in these churches fail to realize that their method of preaching nullifies the effect of the Word of God. If you are operating under any of the aforementioned substitutes, repent and return to God in order to manifest His supernatural power to this generation. The following prayer will help you achieve that:

My Lord Jesus, I repent of replacing Your power with human substitutions. I ask You to fill me once more with Your supernatural power, which I need to carry out Your purpose here on earth.

Ask the Lord to fill you with His power right now!

Balancing Supernatural Power

• Power and character

Character is not a requirement for obtaining a gift, but it is important in pursuing holiness and honoring the Giver of the gift and His gospel. Our character should be formed so that it is able to match the level of power we receive. Only then will we find balance and success. Therefore, it is important to have a mentor—a spiritual mother or father—who can equip and train you in God's supernatural power and also help you to shape and maintain your character.

On the other hand, if we give character more emphasis than power, we turn the gifts of the Holy Spirit into a _reward_ [52]. In other words, they are no longer gifts but rewards or blessings for good behavior. As a man committed to demonstrating the character and power of God, I cannot say that one is less important than the other, but it is a mistake to think that we can be more effective if we dedicate time and effort to shaping our character while setting aside the manifestation of power.

• Power and authority

As we've said, "power" is the Greek word _dynamis_, meaning "strength, power, ability," while the Greek word _exousia_ means "the power of authority (influence) and of right (privilege)…jurisdiction."

Behold, I give you the authority [exousia]…. (Luke 10:19)

When a person has _dynamis_ but lacks _exousia_, he may find himself in a grave situation because of this imbalance. The duration of supernatural power is directly proportional to the level of authority in which a person operates. If you do not _honor_ [53] authority, you might be able to perform miracles, signs, and wonders, but your lack of submission and surrender will begin to manifest in diminished results because the power will expose flaws in the flesh.

When I traveled as an evangelist, I met a pastor in another country who had a church with thousands of members. God was powerfully using him to perform miracles, signs, and wonders, but he did not submit to authority and refused all words of counsel. Eventually, at a time when his church was extremely effective, it was discovered that he was involved in an adulterous affair with a woman from his leadership team. In time, other sinful activities were also discovered in his life. Because of his sin, his ministry was eventually destroyed. Sadly, this is a clear example of what can happen when there is an imbalance of power and authority in your life.

Authority is the ability to exercise the power that leads to Godlike behavior.

• Word and Spirit

For there are three that bear witness in heaven: the Father, the Word, and the Holy Spirit; and these three are one. (1 John 5:7)

When we preach and teach God's Word, we must always wait for the manifestation of the Holy Spirit. An imbalance occurs when people focus only on the Word and never allow the Holy Spirit to move freely, or when they focus only on *manifestations* [54] of power and neglect the priority of the Word. But if we keep these two—the Word and the Spirit—in balance, we will experience the full blessings of God.

It is possible to have an experience and to be deceived, but not having an experience is already a deception.

• Power and harvest

We must understand the relationship between revival and harvest. I define *revival* as "receiving the power to go and gather the harvest of souls." If we fail to gather the harvest, our revival experience has been in *vain* [55]. You are chosen, equipped, and anointed to go throughout the world in search of souls and to perform miracles, signs, and wonders.

• Words and actions

Jesus of Nazareth...was a Prophet mighty in deed and word before God and all the people. (Luke 24:19)

Scripture shows us a Jesus with a double-edged sword in His mouth and seven stars in His right hand, representing both words and actions. (See Revelation 1:16.)

The complete power of the kingdom can manifest only when words and actions are aligned.

Jesus operated in words and actions.

The former account I made, O Theophilus, of all that Jesus began both to do and teach.... (Acts 1:1)

God's Word always shows Jesus...

• *Doing* [56]

• Teaching

Without faith, the kingdom will not have maximum impact.

Believe Me that I am in the Father and the Father in Me, or else believe Me for the sake of the works themselves. (John 14:11)

Theology without works is a dead science.

The multitudes followed Jesus not because they wanted to join a church but to hear about the His kingdom and to see the wonders and miracles He performed. After demonstrating the power, Jesus presented the kingdom. This concept appears over and over again throughout the Gospels.

This has also happened to me in countries where people are reluctant to accept the gospel. Often, the only way to soften their hearts is to demonstrate God's power. After praying for the sick, and after people witness the miracle, they are sensitized and ready for the calling of salvation. They are eager to answer the call, walk to the altar, and receive their salvation.

There are two things we should avoid in our relationship with the Holy Spirit if we want to achieve balance in our character: *grieving* [57] the Holy Spirit and *quenching* [58] Him.

• Do not grieve the Holy Spirit.

And do not grieve the Holy Spirit of God, by whom you were sealed for the day of redemption. (Ephesians 4:30)

In Greek, the word for *"grieve"* is the word *lypeo*, which means "to make sorrowful, to affect with sadness, cause grief, to throw into sorrow...offend."

How do we grieve the Holy Spirit? We do so by having bad or evil attitudes, thoughts, or actions, and by having angry outbursts, slanderous conversations, and bitter quarrels. We also grieve the Holy Spirit when we deliberately participate in sinful activities. When we live in anger, wrath, and deception, we impede the Holy Spirit from flowing through us. Therefore, we grieve Him.

• Do not quench the Holy Spirit.

"Do not quench the Spirit" (1 Thessalonians 5:19).

What does it mean to quench the Holy Spirit?

In Greek, the word for *"quench"* is the word *sbennymi*, meaning "to *extinguish* [59] ...of fire or things on fire...to suppress, stifle." It also implies the idea of obstructing the flow of something—to drown out, kill, or block the source. To quench the Holy Spirit is to cut off His flow and dry up the spring. It is like crimping a hose of running water to stop the flow.

Jesus modeled how we should live with the Holy Spirit
without grieving or quenching Him.

As Christians, we should daily strive not to grieve or quench the Spirit in order to maintain a good relationship with the Holy Spirit.

Grieving the Holy Spirit deals with our character;
quenching the Holy Spirit deals with power.

Power without balance can destroy the user along with those around him. However, if power is used with wisdom and balance, it can impact thousands of lives in positive ways, glorify, and, above all, result in a great harvest of souls.

A ministry that performs miracles but fails to gather the harvest of souls
does not produce anything for the kingdom; it only sensitizes hearts.

3

The Purpose of God's Supernatural Power

Everything created by God has a specific purpose. God never creates anything at random, and He always carries out His plan. In this chapter, we will discover the purpose of God's supernatural power and how to receive and handle it properly.

The Main Objectives of God's Supernatural Power

Jesus did not give us His power in vain. He had clear, specific objectives in mind that are directly related to the _advancement_ [60] of His kingdom on earth. Let us look at eight of those objectives:

1. The formation and edification of Christian character

Character cannot be changed on the basis of personal ideas, concepts, philosophies, achievements, rules, norms, or disciplines. To effect change in character, we need God's supernatural power. Religion—following laws to please God—cannot change man's inner self; this can happen only by God's supernatural grace.

Grace is God's divine power that helps us to obey God and function like Him.

---

2. The development of an effective prayer life

Jesus said, *"The spirit indeed is _willing_ [61], but the flesh is _weak_ [62]"* (Matthew 26:41). Therefore, when your flesh refuses to seek God, you need to ask for His grace to withstand all temptation, and you do this by faith.

3. The fulfillment of ministerial functions and service to God

Serving God effectively is impossible if we depend on our own strength to do it. The preaching and teaching of the gospel must be anointed with supernatural power from God.

4. Victory over sin

We cannot overcome sin in our own strength. Sin was conquered on the cross of Calvary. There, we received the power to live a clean, pure life.

5. The defeat of Satan and his demons

There are two kingdoms in _conflict_ [63]—the kingdom of God and the kingdom of darkness—and we are in the middle of this war. Jesus defeated Satan at the cross, but believers have to take action and manifest that victory on earth.

6. An obedient heart

For I will not dare to speak of any of those things which Christ has not accomplished through me, in word and deed. (Romans 15:18)

We can appeal to people's reason, but this will work for only a short time. The supernatural power of God alone can leave a permanent imprint in their spirit.

7. The ability to achieve great results in a short time

So when they had appointed elders in every church, and prayed with fasting, they commended them to the Lord in whom they had believed. (Acts 14:23)

I estimate that the apostles accomplished this feat in approximately six months. When God's power manifests, it produces an atmosphere in which the Holy Spirit is able to _transform_ (64) and deliver those who have been in churches for a long time without ever experiencing real change.

A message full of God's power can make us advance in minutes to a place that would have taken years to reach in the natural.

---

8. Becoming effective witnesses for Christ

But you shall receive power when the Holy Spirit has come upon you; and you shall be witnesses to Me in Jerusalem, and in all Judea and Samaria, and to the end of the earth. (Acts 1:8)

A witness is someone who personally experiences or acquires knowledge directly from the source and is capable of presenting evidence to prove what he or she saw or heard.

We were created in God's image to do what He does.

When do we receive the power to do what He does? We receive it when we are baptized—or filled—with the Holy Spirit.

Conditions That Must Be Met to Be Filled with the Holy Spirit

According to God's Word, there are three conditions that must be met for us to be filled with the Holy Spirit and to operate in His supernatural power:

*Behold, I send the Promise of My Father upon you; but **tarry** in the city of Jerusalem until you are **endued** with **power** from on high.* (Luke 24:49, emphasis added)

The three conditions have corresponding words to identify them:

- _Tarry_ (65)
- Endued
- Power

Tarry

The Greek word for *"tarry"* is the word *kathizo*, which means "to make to sit down...to settle down." To tarry is to do more than merely wait or sit around doing nothing. The meaning of this word is intimately connected to a degree of authority, for another part of its meaning is "to set, appoint, to confer a kingdom on one." Thus, it is to remain comfortably seated on the throne—our seat of authority through Christ—with a sense of belonging and ownership and with the purpose of exercising authority to reign and to govern.

I have identified three reasons why Jesus calls us to sit on a throne:

1. To *govern* [66] in the political arena with authority

2. To govern in the judicial and legal arena

3. To govern in the spiritual realm

The phrase "to sit on the throne" should be applied in the same manner as it is used where we learn that Jesus is seated on the right hand of the Father. (See, for example, Colossians 3:1; Mark 16:19; Luke 20:42; and Psalm 110:1.)

God...made us sit together in the heavenly places in Christ Jesus.   (Ephesians 2:4, 6)

Jesus taught from God's throne and spoke the Father's words. This is why He taught with such authority. The reason Jesus was resurrected was to ascend to heaven and sit on the throne. From there, He sent us His Holy Spirit. Now, it is our turn, as the body of Christ, to sit on the throne and exercise the same authority.

Endued

The Greek word for *"endued"* is *endyo*, meaning "to sink into (clothing), put on." This refers to the way in which one might dye cloth. It is to be completely covered by a substance that cannot be removed so that it becomes inseparably ours. It is the idea of wearing something until it becomes "a second skin," indissoluble. This is what the anointing of the Holy Spirit does. If we are endued with the resurrected Christ, we become as one with Him. And He gives us the right color according to our personality.

*But **put on** the Lord Jesus Christ, and make no provision for the flesh, to fulfill its lusts.* (Romans 13:14, emphasis added)

***Put on** the whole armor of God, that you may be able to stand against the wiles of the devil.* (Ephesians 6:11, emphasis added)

Are you clothed with *"the whole armor of God"*?

*You have put off the old man with his deeds, and have **put on** the new man who is renewed in knowledge according to the image of Him who created him.* (Colossians 3:9–10, emphasis added)

Have you put on *"the new man"*?

Power

• *Powerful* [67] **(dynamoo)**

The word *dynamoo* is frequently used to describe everything God can do. In the New Testament, however, it is also used to describe what *we* who believe in Him can do. In other words, the Bible places God and His people in the same category—but only after we have been endued by the Holy Spirit with His power. Do not misunderstand me. I am not saying that we are gods or equal to God, but that we can do the _same_ [68] things God does when He imparts us with His power and His grace.

This word denotes the strong ability to do something or to carry out a task. It is to be physically and mentally able to do it, having the natural and logical abilities to do it.

Philippians 4:13 says, *"I can do [ischyo] all things through Christ who strengthens [endynamoo] me."* There are two words used here that relate to *power. Ischyo* means "to have power as shown by extraordinary deeds." If we were to do a literal translation of this verse, it might read, "I am powerfully equipped to do extraordinary deeds through Christ who empowers me."

• Able (*dynamai*)

This word also means "to be able to do something, to be capable, strong and powerful." It describes a person marked by intelligence, knowledge, and ability; one who is highly competent. God is able—*dynamai.*

> *Now to Him Who, by (in consequence of) the [action of His] power [dynamis] that is at work within us, is able [dynamai] to [carry out His purpose and] do superabundantly, far over and above all that we [dare] ask or think [infinitely beyond our highest prayers, desires, thoughts, hopes, or dreams].* (Ephesians 3:20 AMP)

• Possible (*dynatos*)

We find this Greek word fifteen times throughout the Bible. It means "able, powerful, mighty, strong...having power for something." It expresses the _potential_ [69] of something happening according to nature, tradition, or custom; something feasible that can come to pass.

> *Jesus looked at them and said to them, "With men this is impossible, but with God all things are possible."* (Matthew 19:26)

All things are *dynatos* for those who believe.

> *Jesus said to him, "If you can believe, all things are possible to him who believes."* (Mark 9:23)

The word *power*, in all its various forms, appears in Scripture approximately one hundred fifty times with a connotation of explosive power and ability.

- *Power*, as in ability, occurs ninety-five times having to do with God and ninety-five times having to do with the believer.
- *Power*, as in capability, occurs seventy-eight times relating to God being able and seventy-eight times relating to the believer being able.
- *Power*, as in possibility, occurs fifteen times referring to something that is possible for God and fifteen times referring to something that is possible for us.
- *Strengthened* appears sixteen times declaring we are as strong as God, with His strength.
- *Powerfully strong* appears twice declaring that God is powerful and twice declaring how powerful we are in Him.

In the New Testament, we find a large group of Greek words all deriving from the same root word, presented in different contexts, but all—for the most part—translated as *power, dominion, strength, ability,* and *energy.*

In the Bible, Jesus Sent His Disciples in Power

As you go, preach, saying, "The kingdom of heaven is at hand." Heal the sick, cleanse the lepers, raise the dead, cast out demons. Freely you have received, freely give.

(Matthew 10:7–8)

Today, Jesus Continues to Send Us— His Believers—in the Same Power

These signs will follow those who believe: in My name they will cast out demons; they will speak with new tongues. (Mark 16:17)

God is God everywhere. I have preached in more than forty countries, and He has done the same things in all of them. He has never failed, not because I am special but because I make myself *available* [70]. He wants to do it through you, too, if you will make yourself available to Him. He wants you to receive the revelation that you were created in His image and therefore can do the same things that He does. You need only to establish and maintain a close relationship with the Father and receive the infilling of the Holy Spirit. Then, go and preach the Good News everywhere. When you do this, God will confirm His Word.

How to Operate in the Supernatural Power of God

1. Connect to Jesus, the only right source of power.

Jesus said to him, "I am the way, the truth, and the life. No one comes to the Father except through Me." (John 14:6)

Is there a "wrong" source of supernatural power? Many in this present generation are taking the *wrong* [71] paths to find supernatural power: card readers, magic, masonry, the occult, yoga, witchcraft, astrology, horoscopes, tarot cards, telepathy, levitation, mental control, and New Age practices, such as metaphysics, parapsychology, and hypnotism. Some delve into acupuncture, astral projection, Santeria, or reincarnation. Others prefer to dabble in the false religious pursuits of Buddhism, Islam, Hinduism, Hare Krishna, and Rosycrucianism. Still others seek the supernatural through drugs, fame, wealth, prestige, or social status. All of these sources of power are "wrong," and those who practice them will eventually find their lives to be empty and desolate.

2. Change your mind-set.

Do not be conformed to this world, but be transformed by the renewing of your mind, that you may prove what is that good and acceptable and perfect will of God.

(Romans 12:2)

It is essential to renew your mind so that you can have God's perspective and better bring the reality of heaven to earth. A mind that has not been *renewed* (72) is unable to manifest the reality of that power on earth.

3. Learn to flow in power and compassion.

Compassion is heartache motivated by someone else's pain that prompts us to take action by doing something for the one who is suffering.

Compassion without power is sympathy;
power without compassion is professionalism.

The compassion that Jesus felt gave Him the anointing to receive the power, and it motivated Him to take action and accomplish His goal to destroy the works of the devil. Some have received His power before entering into His level of compassion. We must ask the Lord to give us the power and compassion to evangelize, heal the sick, and deliver the captives.

Sympathy is a counterfeit version of compassion.

4

Jesus and the Cross, the Only Legal Source of Supernatural Power

For most of mankind, the cross has become merely a piece of decorative jewelry that is worn around the neck or an ornate piece of lumber displayed in a church. The cross, however, symbolizes everything that Jesus did to carry out God's will on earth and to complete His redeeming work.

The death of Jesus can be divided into three parts:

- Physical torture and death on the cross
- Spiritual death
- Resurrection

Physical Torture and Death on the Cross

Jesus was crucified. Crucifixion is a form of capital punishment carried out by attaching a criminal to a tree. The custom probably started with the Medo-Persian Empire during the reign of the Macedonian king Alexander the Great who is believed to have introduced the practice in Egypt and Carthage. It appears the Romans learned it from the Carthaginians, though it was the Romans who "perfected" this form of torture in a way that produced an agonizingly slow death with a maximum amount of physical and emotional suffering. It was truly one of the cruelest, most humiliating methods of execution, reserved specifically for slaves, murderers, traitors, and the vilest of criminals. Roman law protected its citizens from crucifixion, except for army deserters. For Israelites, a person who was crucified was seen as a *curse* [73].

If a man has committed a sin deserving of death, and he is put to death, and you hang him on a tree...for he who is hanged is accursed of God. (Deuteronomy 21:22–23)

Specific Steps That Led to Jesus' Physical Death

- **He was *whipped*.** [74] (Mark 15:15)

In Jesus' day, the whip was an instrument commonly used to inflict punishment. It was usually composed of several woven belts with small pieces of lead and sharp pieces of bone or sheep's teeth. To undergo the punishment, the criminal was undressed, tied to a pillar, and flogged. The lashes were directed toward the back, torso, and legs, and the severity of each lash depended on which part of the body it made contact with. The intent of the punisher was to weaken the victim to the point of passing out. Traditionally, this punishment was accompanied by verbal scorn and mockery. As the torture was applied, the cuts went deeper and deeper, causing increased damage to the muscle. The extreme pain and massive loss of blood often led to death due to circulatory shock.

> [Jesus] *Himself bore our sins in His own body on the tree.* (1 Peter 2:24)

- **His beard was plucked out.**

> *I gave My back to those who struck Me, and My cheeks to those who plucked out the beard; I did not hide My face from shame and spitting.* (Isaiah 50:6)

Plucking out the beard or hair was a major insult in Middle Eastern culture because the beard was a sign of virility and masculine dignity.

- **His face was *spat* (75) upon.**

> *Then they spat in His face and beat Him; and others struck Him with the palms of their hands.* (Matthew 26:67)

For Jews, spitting in the presence of others was an insult; spitting on someone was an even more grievous affront. When the Roman guards spit on Jesus' face, that was even worse.

- **He was forced to wear a crown of thorns.**

> *And the soldiers twisted a crown of thorns and put it on His head.* (John 19:2)

The crown of thorns was woven of thorn branches normally used to light fires. It is believed that the crown had more than three rows of thorns, and that it may have been shaped like a helmet, covering Jesus' head from the neck to the forehead.

Jesus' Health

It can be assumed that Jesus was in good health as He faced His twelve-hour ordeal and that He was not suffering from either an illness or a weak constitution. To evaluate His health, we must take into account the merciless punishment He received after the Jewish trial, the emotional stress caused by the abandonment of His closest disciples, and the rejection He experienced at the hands of the people who had praised Him only a few days before.

Agony and Physical Death on the Cross

As was customary, the condemned man was made to carry his own cross from the place where he was whipped to the place outside of the city walls where he would be crucified. Historians maintain that the weight of these crosses was almost always over three hundred pounds. The gallows, or horizontal crosspiece, alone probably weighed between seventy-five and one hundred twenty-five pounds.

After all the pain of the torture He had endured, Jesus' clothing was removed, and He was finally placed on the cross in an uncomfortable position that made breathing difficult. Added to this were dehydration caused by the loss of blood; fever, which only increased his thirst; the further humiliation of His naked suffering; and the scoffing and insults of a bloodthirsty crowd. If the Roman guard took pity on the victim, he might offer him a mixture of wine and myrrh, which served as a mild anesthetic. According to Scripture, Jesus *refused* (76) this. (See Mark 15:23.)

At the moment of crucifixion, the criminal was thrown to the ground on his back. His arms were extended and were either nailed or tied to the gallows, the legs to the post. Apparently, Romans preferred nails to rope. Recently, archeologists discovered a crucified body dating back to the days of Jesus in an ossuary close to the city of Jerusalem. They uncovered sharp iron nails approximately seven inches long and one inch in diameter.

> *I am poured out like water, and all My bones are out of joint; My heart is like wax; it has melted within Me. My strength is dried up like a potsherd, and My tongue clings to My jaws; You have brought Me to the dust of death.* (Psalm 22:14–15)

Eventually, excess blood accumulated in the heart, blocking circulation, which, combined with the fever caused by trauma, tetanus, and exhaustion, often killed the victim in a matter of days or hours. In order to accelerate death, it was customary to break the offender's *legs* (77) with a hammer, eliminating the ability of the victim to push up with the feet in order to breathe. On other occasions, the offender was pierced with a sword or spear or was asphyxiated with smoke.

Jesus suffered all of that in our place. He allowed Himself to be treated as if He were the worst of criminals in order to redeem us from our sins. When we read the biblical account of this event, we realize the immense love God has for us—an unconditional love. Jesus died so that we could be free from sin and condemnation. If anyone doubts God's love, please, look to the cross and observe the interchange that was produced there out of love.

This was the physical death Jesus suffered. Now, let us consider His spiritual death.

Spiritual Death

Jesus' physical and spiritual deaths were both set into motion in the garden of Gethsemane. There, God the Father provided the Lamb that would redeem mankind from all its sins. Jesus was the Lamb without sin or blemish who offered his life for humanity. No one can fathom how the Son of God—pure and holy and without sin—suddenly agreed to take upon Himself the filthy *sins* (78) of the world. This is why, in the garden, He pleaded,

> *O My Father, if it is possible, let this cup pass from Me; nevertheless, not as I will, but as You will.* (Matthew 26:39)

If you consider that the pain suffered by Jesus on the cross was horrible, His spiritual suffering was even greater. He was not as concerned about His physical death as He was with the cup the Father gave Him to drink. Can you perceive the content of the cup? It was full of *iniquity* (79), the wickedness of mankind throughout time, ages, and generations. It contained the sins of resentment, homosexuality, hate, lies, rejection, generational curses, theft, abortion, murder, sexual abuse, sickness, idolatry, witchcraft, Satanism, and much more. Jesus didn't just become sin, however; He also became the root of wickedness, or what the Bible refers to in Romans 7:18 as the *"sinful nature"* (NIV). It was in this condition that He climbed on the cross and from there He shouted, *"My God, My God, why have You forsaken Me?"* (Matthew 27:46).

This was the first and final time that Father and Son would be separated by the barrier of man's iniquity. This was not a moment of communion for them, as martyrism was for Christian saints, who, as they were being stoned, burned, or devoured by lions, were often said to have been filled with God's peace and grace, which brought comfort and allowed them to die in peace. This is not what happened to Jesus. He was left completely alone, separated from the Father's presence and deprived of His grace. God abandoned Jesus precisely when the Son needed His Father most. When we understand this, we can begin to love God more and to hate sin as He hates it.

So when Jesus had received the sour wine, He said, "It is finished!" (John 19:30)

In Greek, the word for *"finished"* is *teleo*, meaning "to bring to a close, to finish, to end; to perform, execute, complete, fulfill." Jesus said, in effect, "The debt has been satisfied completely; there is no more debt." These words were not a cry of pain or anguish but of *victory* [80], like a gladiator after winning a death match.

Resurrection from the Dead

Sin [81] and death had been conquered, but there were still things that needed to be done. Jesus had to go to hell and pay for our sins because that is what God's justice demanded. There, He took the keys of hell and death from Satan. The sting of death could not hold Him any longer. God the Father raised Him from the dead so He could sit on the throne of glory. God gave Him all power and authority over heaven and earth. Then, Jesus gave us the same power and authority to go in His name and proclaim the gospel of the kingdom throughout the world.

The Revelation of the Cross

The cross is the sacrifice offered by Jesus in place of the human race, with all of its consequences and benefits. The cross implies two fundamental roles for the Son of God:

• **Jesus was the** *priest* [82] **who offered the sacrifice.**

For such a High Priest was fitting for us…who does not need daily, as those high priests, to offer up sacrifices, first for His own sins and then for the people's, for this He did once for all when He offered up Himself. (Hebrews 7:26–27)

• **Jesus was the** *sacrifice* [83]

…how much more shall the blood of Christ, who through the eternal Spirit offered Himself without spot to God. (Hebrews 9:13–14)

The cross is the basis of God to provide absolute and total provision to mankind.

Everything we need, now and in the future—mentally, emotionally, materially, financially, or spiritually, be it power, authority, love, health, healing, or anything else—was provided at the cross. There is no other source.

The cross is the only genuine source of supernatural power.

It is time for the church to preach the message of the cross. It must be given the highest priority. We cannot diminish the cross.

God told the nation of Israel to leave Egypt, and to raise an altar. They were not to place anything around it—not trees, decorations, or any objects that might separate the people from His presence. Let this be our example. We cannot surround the message of the cross with anything that robs it of power or diminishes the _supremacy_ [84] of Jesus. No religion in the world can equal the message of the cross.

The Cross: Abstract or Reality?

When we stop placing the cross at the center of our message, our faith loses its meaning and we end up in bondage to traditions, regulations, and laws which are impossible to obey.

What Supernatural Power Did Jesus Loosen at the Cross?

O foolish Galatians!...Are you so foolish? Having begun in the Spirit, are you now being made perfect by the flesh?
(Galatians 3:1, 3)

On the cross, Jesus loosened the supernatural _grace_ [85] of God. When we act without God's grace, we become _legalistic_ [86]. This is what happened to the Galatians. The same is happening to the church today. Hence, there is an absence of power.

How does the enemy react to the work at the cross? Satan counterattacks the work of Jesus at the cross with the spirit of witchcraft. His goal is to darken the cross by provoking carnality, legalism, and paganism.

What Is Legalism?

Legalism is the human effort to carry out the law in ones strength. It is an attempt to become holy or righteous through rules, traditions, and _laws_ [87]. It adds other elements to the requisites established by God that lead to righteousness. God only asks that we believe, since we are justified by faith in Jesus and in His redeeming work at the cross.

Christ has redeemed us from the curse of the law, having become a curse for us.
(Galatians 3:13)

When a person trusts in his own strength to obtain salvation or to receive God's blessings, he automatically falls under the curse of the Galatians.

Legalism leads to witchcraft, and witchcraft leads to people falling under a curse.

The Two Great Works of the Cross

• **What the cross did *for* us**

Let us take a moment to consider the perfect work at the cross. The last words Jesus pronounced on the cross were, "It is _finished_ [88]" (John 19:30). In effect, He said, "It is perfectly and completely done. It is done in eternity."

• **What the cross did *in* us**

The essence of the cross consists in that Jesus took our place. He personally suffered the totality of the punishment that we deserved for our disobedience. In exchange, we received all the goodness that Jesus received for His obedience.

The Divine Exchange

This exchange came about in the following way:

• **Jesus was wounded so we could be** *forgiven* [89].

But He was wounded for our transgressions, He was bruised for our iniquities.

(Isaiah 53:5)

• **Jesus carried our sickness and suffered our sorrows so we could receive healing.**

Surely He has borne our griefs and carried our sorrows. (Isaiah 53:4)

Every time the Bible mentions the cross and the redeeming work that took place upon it, *sickness* [90] is connected to it. However, it is always mentioned in past tense indicating that healing already took place in eternity. Now, all we have to do is to appropriate the health that Jesus offers.

• **Jesus became sin and carried our sinful nature so we could be justified.**

For He made Him who knew no sin to be sin for us, that we might become the righteousness of God in Him. (2 Corinthians 5:21)

• **Jesus died in our place so we can share in His eternal life.**
• **Jesus carried our curse so we could be blessed.**
• **Jesus paid for our poverty so we could be prosperous.**

Yet for your sakes He became poor, that you through His poverty might become rich.

(2 Corinthians 8:9)

• **Jesus suffered our shame so we could partake of His glory.**

...bringing many sons to glory... (Hebrews 2:10)

• **Jesus suffered our rejection so we could be** *accepted* [91] **in Him.**

---

*Rejection is one of the deepest wounds the human soul can experience,
but Jesus suffered it on the cross.*

How can we appropriate the benefits of the cross? By faith. Therefore, there are no substitutions for living by faith. We can trust in God's character and believe that He is righteous, just, and faithful and will keep all of His promises.

...through whom also we have access by faith into this grace in which we stand.

(Romans 5:2)

What Are the Benefits of the Cross?

- **The cross delivered us from the "old man."**

Our old man was crucified with Him. (Romans 6:6)

The *"old man"* is our sinful Adamic nature. It can be summed up in one word: <u>rebellion</u> [92]. We all carry a rebellious being within us. We were born this way because we were conceived and formed in iniquity. (See Psalm 51:5.) The only way to defeat this rebellious man is execution—a sentence that has already been carried out at the cross. This historic event is real and unchanging. Knowing and understanding this event will make you free.

- **The cross delivered us from "self."**

The ego is the part of the soul where the "self" dwells. It is where "I want" and "I think" can be found. Many people choose not to surrender to Jesus out of <u>selfishness</u> [93] because they are afraid to leave their family, wealth, position, comfort, and sense of security.

Ego is the greatest obstacle keeping us from carrying out God's will.

One manifestation of ego or self is egocentrism, or selfishness. This is equivalent to thinking that the world revolves around us. It is believing that we are the center of attention and that other people don't deserve to be appreciated or esteemed at the same level as we do. It also means that Jesus exists to please us, rather than our existing to please Him. A few manifestations of self or ego that need to be sacrificed are: pride, personal ambition, radical nationalism, sectarianism, and racism. What is the remedy for ego? The answer is the <u>cross</u> [94]. Every ministry, man, or woman who fails to submit to the principle of the cross risks becoming corrupted. When you apply the cross to your ego, Satan cannot touch you. The cross is the only safe place to be.

The more I humble myself, the more power God manifests through me.

- **The cross delivered us from the flesh.**

Then He said to them all, "If anyone desires to come after Me, let him deny himself, and take up his cross daily, and follow Me." (Luke 9:23)

The flesh always acts independently of God's will. The only requirement to live in the flesh is to do our own will.

- **The cross delivered us from the <u>world</u> [95].**

But God forbid that I should boast except in the cross of our Lord Jesus Christ, by whom the world has been crucified to me, and I to the world. (Galatians 6:14)

Regardless of what God says in His Word, most believers live under duress by the world's system—by its power, comfort, material rewards, fears, and anxieties.

The Bible commands us not to allow the world to mold us according to its standards. To avoid this, we must reject the worldly mentality and begin to renew our minds until we can think like God thinks.

• **The cross delivered us from Satan's power and authority.**

Having disarmed principalities and powers, He made a public spectacle of them, triumphing over them in it.
(Colossians 2:15)

On the cross, Jesus defeated the devil. This victory is irrevocable, eternal, and _permanent_ [96]. Satan cannot do anything to change it. If we come in contact with the enemy on any subject other than the cross, we can be defeated. But if we confront him at the cross, we will always be victorious. Satan cannot change the work that was done at the cross. It is eternal. However, he can camouflage it and diminish its power, and that is the direction, or goal, of his strategies.

What Message Should We Preach for the Power of God to Be Loosened?

We preach Christ crucified.
(1 Corinthians 1:23)

Many churches have substituted the message of the cross with other messages that neither transform nor edify the people, messages that are incapable of producing miracles because they lack power.

The only message capable of loosening God's supernatural power is the message of the cross.

Why does God's power seem absent from many lives and ministries? Why are the sick not healed? Why do the blind not recover their sight? Why are the lame not walking? Why are we not seeing cancer dry up and disappear? There is only one answer to these questions: because we are not _preaching_ [97] the message of the cross.

Because the foolishness of God is wiser than men, and the weakness of God is stronger than men.
(1 Corinthians 1:25)

The cross is the true source of wisdom and power.

Without the power of the cross, we can teach good morals, practice good Christian ethics, have good intentions, and even preach good sermons, but we cannot produce a changed or transformed heart. But if we preach the message of the cross—Christ crucified and resurrected—we will see God's supernatural power confirmed with miracles, signs, and wonders.

5

Faith: The First Dimension of the Supernatural

The supernatural dimension is an eternal realm—invisible, permanent, and unchanging. It is where all things exist and are complete, the perennial "now" that can be accessed only by faith. If we want to know and move in the supernatural, we need revelation and understanding of the three dimensions. This is a fundamental requirement for receiving supernatural power from a supernatural God. The three dimensions of the supernatural are:

- Faith

- Anointing

- Glory

This chapter will be an in-depth study of faith. The next two chapters will cover the dimensions of anointing and glory.

In the body of Christ, legitimate movements of the Holy Spirit have blessed thousands of people. In every move of the Spirit, there are always some who will take a truth to the _extreme_ [98] until it becomes a stronghold, then, a dogma, until, finally, it becomes a complete impediment to any move of the Spirit. Faith is one of those truths that can be misunderstood. Some people think they live by faith when, in truth, they are far from doing so. In many cases, faith has been reduced to something natural when it should be supernatural. With this in mind, I will begin by defining what faith is not.

Faith is not presumption or optimism. These things can resemble faith, but they are not faith.

What Is Faith?

Now faith is the substance of things hoped for, the evidence of things not seen.

(Hebrews 11:1)

The word _"faith"_ is the Hebrew word _emunah_, meaning "firmness, steadfastness, _fidelity_ [99]." As you can see, each of these meanings describes an aspect of God's nature. And they have nothing to do with presumption, hope, or optimism. The factor that assures us that the Lord will act is that God cannot lie or fail to keep His word. If He said it, you can rest assured that it will be as He said.

- **Faith is the mind of the Holy Spirit revealed to man that he might operate and have dominion in this dimension of time, space, and matter.**

Now faith is the assurance (the confirmation, the title deed) of the things [we] hope for, being the proof of things [we] do not see and the conviction of their reality [faith perceiving as real fact what is not revealed to the senses]. (Hebrews 11:1 AMP)

A more literal translation from the Greek would be: "Now faith is the reality of the foundation where hope takes root, or is established. It is the reality of all that exists, and it exercises control and dominion over the things we cannot see."

Faith is the divine ability given to man to go beyond the natural realm. As I said earlier, if God had planned for man to live only in the natural dimension, He never would have given him faith. God created the natural realm. He dwells in and out of it, but He is not bound by it. God set time in motion, but when He created man, He placed a yearning for eternity within him, thereby enabling man to live in both dimensions—the natural and the supernatural. The invisible spiritual realm is superior to, and has dominion over, the natural realm.

The Natural Realm

Mankind attempts to define God according to the *natural* (100) realm in which he lives, but God is much more than time, space, and matter. The breakthrough will come when we begin to operate by faith.

Do not be conformed to this world (this age), [fashioned after and adapted to its external, superficial customs]. (Romans 12:2 AMP)

For us, the natural realm is reality, but in God's mind, this dimension is subject to being cursed. Nature is devastated by the curse that was put upon it after the fall and cries out for God's children to manifest the supernatural. We cannot get comfortable in one *dimension* (101) that is always changing. Our faith needs absolute, unchanged values, like Jesus, His kingdom, and His Word.

Everything to which you conform will become your reality.

What Is the Difference Between the Natural and Supernatural Realms?

The natural dimension is like a straight line that has a beginning and an end. Eternity is a circle; it has neither a beginning nor an end. When you enter eternity, everything is. This is God's habitat, where time does not exist.

For thus says the High and Lofty One who inhabits eternity. (Isaiah 57:15)

Faith allows us to cross the limits of time and reach *eternity* (102). In the spiritual realm, everything is finished and complete. Everything was provided for by Jesus at the cross. How can we manifest these things on earth? The only way to do it is by faith.

What Does the Natural Realm Represent?

We need to be free of the bondage that keeps us subject to the _senses_ (103)—free, so we do not have to smell, feel, taste, hear, or see to believe. When we understand faith, the impossible becomes possible because faith has dominion and control over the laws of time, space, and matter. For example, when we go to refinance our house, the bank establishes that it will take thirty years to finish paying off the mortgage. Due to interest on the loan, by the end of those thirty years, we will have paid four times the value of the house. In this case, the one who determined the time to complete payments on the house was the bank. But what if we determine the time by exercising our faith and paying off the mortgage in only five years? Then, by faith, we allow God to supernaturally bring into the natural realm the resources we need to keep us from being enslaved by a debt for a longer period of time. In other words, we allow God to deliver His divine provision. If we do this, we break the laws of time. We submit to the provision, not the debt!

- **Faith is now.**

When is faith due? Faith is now! Faith is the past and the future together in the present, constituting the now.

And God said to Moses, "I AM WHO I AM." (Exodus 3:14)

God does not need time. He dwells in the _now_ (104). He does not need the day or the night to do His works because the supernatural realm—the past and the future—come together in the present. From God's standpoint, His future can invade the present. One reason we do not see supernatural manifestations—miracles, signs, and wonders—in the church is because these things take place in the _now,_ while we live our lives waiting for things to happen in the future. Faith compresses time. Therefore, what would normally take a year can now be done in one day. Everything works according to our faith.

**Faith is God's radar in the believer to determine the distance and time between the natural and supernatural, the visible and invisible.**

You will also declare a thing, and it will be established for you; so light will shine on your ways. (Job 22:28)

**Faith is not in the future because faith is not going to be; faith is now.**

Most believers know where they come from. Some know where they are going. But few believe what they are _now._ They are unaware of what God is doing and saying _now._ When we abandon faith to live according to sight only, the enemy makes us focus on the _problems_ (105), infirmities, and difficulties. But let us remember that these things are temporal; they are passing away and dying each second. Sickness is passing. Poverty is passing. Oppression and depression are passing. By faith, we must believe that God is intervening _now._

Now is the time to activate our faith. Right now, let's declare and establish the time and distance to receive healing for cancer or any other sickness we might have. Let's declare the money we need and when it will appear supernaturally. When we speak, there is matter—raw material—in our mouths to create by His Word and to activate by faith.

The Definition of Faith Is in the Now

If we take this definition of faith, we will begin to see things as God sees them.

I am God, and there is none like Me, declaring the end from the beginning, and from ancient times things that are not yet done. (Isaiah 46:9–10)

When faith touches things that cannot be seen, it gives us *conviction* [106] and persuades us to wait for them. Faith converts things that cannot be seen into something certain, something real. This happens in the *now,* not in the future. If we read the definition of faith in a logical way, we will notice that there is still something pending, something that has yet to manifest, something that waits for the future. But remember that in eternity, God already did it. He has already formed new organs and bones. He has already healed incurable diseases and performed creative miracles. What is our part in all of this? All we need to do is appropriate the miracle by faith, *now*!

Being confident of this very thing, that He who has begun a good work in you will complete it until the day of Jesus Christ. (Philippians 1:6)

God started creating us in eternity and finished us before giving us the shape and form we have today. We arrived in the *now* via God's faith. Therefore, we don't have to seek faith, because God already gave it to us to receive all that He *promised* [107]. We will believe what we can't see only if we see it through the faith of the One who sees. God sees our healing, prosperity, and happiness because He already did it all.

• **Faith feeds on impossibilities.**

A believer full of God's supernatural faith is passionate about the impossible, and his faith is fed when he confronts "impossible" situations. When God gave each one of us a measure of faith, an appetite for the impossible came into our spirit. We were created to have this appetite for the impossible.

• **Faith perceives as real that which has yet to be revealed to the natural senses.**

The nature of faith is not to be revealed to the *senses* [108]. When God commands that we do something, it might not make sense.

• **God gave each person a measure of faith.**

God has dealt to each one a measure of faith. (Romans 12:3)

The Word confirms that everyone has faith but not in the same measure. When we take our measure of faith to the limit, God takes us to a higher level. It is possible to lose that measure of faith instead of gaining more if we choose to remain comfortable at a place where our faith is not challenged. If we are being good stewards with the measure of faith we have, God will give us more.

What is a measure of faith? What does Scripture say about this? A measure of faith is the sphere of *influence* [109] and the level of authority where we place our faith to produce.

It is my firm belief that one human being is capable of influencing—for good or evil—an average of around ten thousand people in his or her lifetime.

Because everyone has been given a measure of faith,
there will never be an excuse to not believe in God.

How Do We Receive God's Faith?

So Jesus answered and said to them, "Have faith in God." (Mark 11:22)

A more literal translation for this verse is, "Have God's faith." In Greek, the verb is in the passive voice, which means that the action comes from outside. In other words, Jesus does not ask us to have faith in God, but God gives us a measure of faith that belongs to Him. In other words, our human nature is _incapable_ [110] of generating faith on its own. We must take hold of God's faith.

Human nature can doubt but not believe; divine nature can believe but not doubt.

In essence, Jesus was telling Peter, "Receive God's faith to bless others." Later, in Acts, we see Peter saying the same thing.

Then Peter said, "Silver and gold I do not have, but what I do have I give you: In the name of Jesus Christ of Nazareth, rise up and walk." (Acts 3:6)

The power of God in the realm of miracles is called faith.

Let's study this in more detail:

• **God gave Abraham "dynamite" faith.**

[Abraham] *did not waver at the promise of God through unbelief, but was strengthened* [*endynamoo*] *in faith, giving glory to God.* (Romans 4:20)

Abraham's faith needed strengthening. *Endynamoo*—or God's "dynamite"—had to come upon him. As a human being, Abraham did not have the faith he needed. Therefore, God had to fill him with His faith to help him wait for the son God promised. When God finished strengthening Abraham, he was _persuaded_ [111] and convicted to wait for the certainty of his *now*.

[Abraham was] *fully convinced that what He had promised He was also able to perform.* (Romans 4:21)

When we have God's faith,
His Word in our mouth is the same as it is in His mouth.

• **God used "dynamite" in Sarah's womb.**

By faith Sarah herself also received strength to conceive seed, and she bore a child when she was past the age, because she judged Him faithful who had promised.

(Hebrews 11:11)

How Do We Receive God's Faith?

God's faith to believe as He believes is received by saying, "Lord, I open my heart so You can fill it with Your dynamite faith. Destroy in me all doubt, unbelief, reasoning, and argumentation so I may receive the miracles You promised me, and so that I may give to others the faith You have imparted into my life."

What Are the Enemies of Faith?

• *Unbelief* (112)

Beware, brethren, lest there be in any of you an evil heart of unbelief in departing from the living God.

(Hebrews 3:12)

Unbelief is a wicked spirit that uses reason to make us refuse or oppose God. In addition, we now have to deal with "educated unbelief." What does this mean? Educated unbelief tries to supplant the spiritual man. To accomplish this, scientific, philosophical, and psychological arguments are developed for the sole purpose of eliminating faith. Unbelief has become the means through which we measure our reality.

The only biblical reason to fail is unbelief.

Truth is the highest level of reality, and it may be understood only by *revelation* (113) Jesus is truth. When God speaks, what He says is truth, and it will come to pass, regardless of circumstances or what theologians, doctors, or the devil may say.

Truth is the highest level of reality.

• **Human reason**

By faith we understand that the worlds were framed.

(Hebrews 11:3)

"By faith we understand." Note that *faith* (114) comes first and then *understanding* (115). To believe God with human reasoning doesn't make sense, and it will never increase our level of faith. The enemy's goal is to keep us within the limits of reason, as he did to Adam in the garden of Eden. This is why, each time we seek to understand God through reason, we once again eat of the tree of the knowledge of good and evil.

When I say that reason is the enemy of faith, or the supernatural, it is because I want us to understand a very important point: reason, or intellect, has its place and should be used in the physical world to make wise decisions in the natural realm. God gave us the ability to reason for a specific purpose. Therefore, it is good to use reason within the natural realm. However, if we try using it in the spiritual realm, it will not work.

Faith is the ability given to every believer to believe the unreasonable.

Everything God did, as recorded in the Bible, appears *unreasonable* [116] to human reason. Let us look at the following examples:

• **Shadrach, Meshach, and Abed-Nego were cast into the fire but not burned.**

"Look!" he answered, "I see four men loose, walking in the midst of the fire; and they are not hurt, and the form of the fourth is like the Son of God." (Daniel 3:25)

• **Abraham fathered his descendants in his old age.**

No longer shall your name be called Abram, but your name shall be Abraham; for I have made you a father of many nations. (Genesis 17:5)

• **Noah built an ark.**

By faith Noah, being divinely warned of things not yet seen, moved with godly fear, prepared an ark for the saving of his household, by which he condemned the world and became heir of the righteousness which is according to faith. (Hebrews 11:7)

In the absence of reason, faith says, "Now." In the presence of faith, God acts now.

Faith cannot be *judged* [117] or proven in a court of law where reason rules because there are no books or codes that can judge faith. Jurisprudence judges on the basis of human reasoning and deals only with facts, tangible acts that can be proven on the basis of our five natural senses—sight, smell, taste, hearing, and touch. A court of law has no room for faith.

If a doctor diagnoses a sickness, even when God's Word says we are healed, the human verdict will most often be sickness because this deals with two different realms: the natural and the supernatural. The more time we spend trying to reason what God wants to do in and through us, the more we will lose the manifestation of the supernatural—His miracles and blessings.

No Bible story makes sense until God comes on the scene.

Renewing our minds is a process by which we substitute God's logic for our human reason. Only then are we able to realize that everything He does makes sense.

In the absence of reason, all things are possible.
When faith is present, even the impossible is made possible.

How to Cross Over from Reason to Faith

To live by faith, we must *disconnect* [118] our reasoning ability and "loose" our minds. If we believe our minds, we will believe only in man-made reason and will doubt God's power. Faith doesn't need human reasoning to believe because it supersedes reasoning and is not based on common sense.

The realm of the impossible is founded on human logic and established in human reason.

How Do We Rise from One Dimension of Faith to a Greater One?

For in [the gospel] *the righteousness of God is revealed from faith to faith; as it is written, "The just shall live by faith."*   (Romans 1:17)

To go *"from faith to faith"* is to go from one dimension or degree of faith to another. This indicates that the movement does not begin at the point of departure, but it takes off from a place already advanced.

The level of revelation in an individual determines the measure of faith in which he will operate.

If revealed knowledge ceases, faith also ceases. It will decelerate and enter into the natural realm. We cannot believe in something we do not know. This means that we cannot allow faith to become *stagnant* [119]. Faith must be in constant movement.

If our faith is not kept active, nothing will happen. Is it possible to be stuck in a dimension of faith? Yes, it is possible, and there are clear signs that show when our faith has become inactive. For example, when nothing new happens in church, when the congregation ceases to grow, when signs, miracles, and wonders cease, or when God's presence is nowhere to be found, our faith has stopped growing. He wants us to advance to a greater level, but for that to happen, we need revelation to pave the way to a new dimension. If we want to walk in the *now*, we cannot ignore God's revelation for this time. We cannot walk in the present truth with yesterday's revelation because faith is *now*, always in the present.

To have faith in the now, we must have a revelation of the present truth.

You know and are established in the present truth.   (2 Peter 1:12)

Truth is present, and faith is *now*. If yesterday's faith were sufficient, the Bible would not command that we go *"from faith to faith."* God wants to do something new and fresh *now*! Faith has an expiration date. If it is not *now*, it is not faith. Furthermore, yesterday's revelation is worthless when we try to activate it now. What used to work no longer works. Therefore, God motivates us to take up a new dimension and revelation.

6

The Anointing: The Second Dimension of the Supernatural

The previous chapter covered the first of the three dimensions that make up the supernatural. Now, let us learn about the anointing.

What Is the Anointing?

The anointing is the ability God gives the believer to accomplish the work of the ministry and to serve Him. The physical act of anointing is to apply oil on someone for the purpose of consecrating the work of God in his or her life. It is a confirmation of a calling or function, sealed by the Holy Spirit, in which the *oil* [120] is only a visible symbol. The person who anoints another is God's agent. This person applies the oil, but God is the One who sends His Holy Spirit. Since the earliest of times, anointing has been the way to seal the consecration of God on people who are called to carry out special functions, for example, kings and priests. Through the act of anointing, the person is enabled to carry out the assigned functions.

The anointing is God doing His work through our humanity.

In the area of ministry, supernatural power is called the *holy anointing.*

I have found My servant David; with My holy oil I have anointed him. (Psalm 89:20)

Today, a variety of oils are used for the purpose of anointing, but with Moses, God gave specific instructions on how to prepare the oil of the holy *anointing* [121]

Also take for yourself quality spices—five hundred shekels of liquid myrrh, half as much sweet-smelling cinnamon (two hundred and fifty shekels), two hundred and fifty shekels of sweet-smelling cane, five hundred shekels of cassia, according to the shekel of the sanctuary, and a hin of olive oil. And you shall make from these a holy anointing oil, an ointment compounded according to the art of the perfumer. It shall be a holy anointing oil. (Exodus 30:23–25)

God specified which ingredients to use, each representing a prophetic symbol of something that was to come in the New Testament.

- **Myrrh**

Myrrh is a bitter herb with a sweet aroma. It represents suffering, pain, anguish, distress, death, trials, tribulations, and persecution. Myrrh represents the price we pay for the anointing. Many desire the anointing but are not willing to pay the price to have it.

I have suffered...that I may know Him and the power of His resurrection, and the fellowship of His sufferings, being conformed to His death. (Philippians 3:8, 10)

- **Cinnamon**

Cinnamon represents firmness and stability. These elements are applied to Christian character and are fundamental to operating in the anointing.

- **Cane**

Cane, or calamus in the King James Version, is a long, straight reed with green and red coloring that smells a bit like ginger. It is associated with the gifts of the Holy Spirit and divine authority. This is indicative that the anointing flows in us when submit to authority.

- **Cassia**

Cassia is a sweet-smelling bush of yellow flowers. The leaves of this plant are dried and pulverized to prepare the anointing oil. The word "cassia" derives from a root word that means "to bow down out of honor and reverence." Therefore, the cassia flower represents prayer, praise, and worship.

- **Oil**

The oil for the anointing is extracted from the *olive* (122) tree, and it represents the Holy Spirit. The anointing has two important characteristics: it is a tangible substance that can be applied with a cloth or by pouring from a pot or jar, and it is transferable from one person to another.

What Was the Purpose of the Oil of the Holy Anointing?

In the Jewish temple, the oil of the holy anointing was used to anoint the tabernacle, the holy utensils, and the priests so that they could be consecrated, identified, and prepared to enter into God's presence.

With it you shall anoint the tabernacle of meeting and the ark of the Testimony.
(Exodus 30:26)

In the tabernacle, no one could touch an instrument or utensil unless he had been anointed because the anointing is what prepares an individual to stand safely in God's presence. This is also true for us today. God first anoints us with His holy anointing and then *consecrates* (123) and sanctifies us in preparation to receive His glory.

What Is the Difference Between Talent and Anointing?

Many people trust and depend solely on their talents. Thus, when they praise, worship, and serve God, they do not do so wholeheartedly. Doing these things has nothing to do with talent but with how anointed one is. I have seen people with little talent bring God's presence like no one else when they praise.

The anointing of the Holy Spirit is a deposit to receive God's glory.

In Him you also...were sealed with the Holy Spirit of promise. (Ephesians 1:13)

When the measures and the gifts unite, God's glory descends. Otherwise, His glorty will not come. Let us now analyze two types of the anointing:

• **Personal anointing**

But to each one of us grace was given according to the measure of Christ's gift.

(Ephesians 4:7)

Personal anointing is the _measure_ (124) of supernatural grace that God gives each believer to enable him or her to fulfill his or her calling.

• **Corporate anointing**

...till we all come to the unity of the faith and of the knowledge of the Son of God, to a perfect man, to the measure of the stature of the fullness of Christ. (Ephesians 4:13)

A corporate anointing is an anointing of the Holy Spirit that is poured out when all personal measures are collected and when everyone becomes as one in Christ. God always commands us to seek unity and depend on one another, according to our measure, in order to become powerful on earth, just as Jesus is.

What Is a Mantle?

The word _mantle_ (125) has several meanings, including "a loose sleeveless garment worn over other clothes...a figurative cloak symbolizing preeminence or authority." In all its meanings, the mantle represents a covering, or protection.

The mantle, or anointing, is our covering while we reside on earth.

In the spiritual realm, the word *mantle* also means "glory, kindness, lordship, excellence, nobility, authority, strength, essence, and great courage."

The Two Mantles of Jesus

• **The mantle of His deity, which is His glory**

Christ Jesus,...being in the form of God, did not consider it robbery to be equal with God, but made Himself of no reputation. (Philippians 2:5, 6–7)

Before coming to earth, Jesus took of His mantle of glory. He came like any other man, anointed by the Holy Spirit but without His mantle of glory, which He had willingly left behind in heaven.

- **The mantle of His humanity, which is His anointing**

For He whom God has sent speaks the words of God, for God does not give the Spirit by measure. (John 3:34)

Jesus defeated the devil and his demons in the form of a common man but with the anointing of the HOly Spirit. With His anointing, He healed the sick, blind, and deaf; He rebuked demons; and He raised the dead—not as God but as a *man* [126] full of the Holy Spirit. If Jesus did this, we can do it, too. As a matter of fact, Jesus promised that we should do greater things than He! (See John 14:12.)

Impartation takes place due to a direct *intervention* [127] of the Holy Spirit. He takes the gift of one individual and gives a measure to others who desperately seek it. Is it transference from one to another? Yes, it is a mystery that allows gifts to reach others. How can we impart gifts or virtue to others? Through books, preaching, teachings, prophecies, God's Word, the laying on of hands, and even anointed cloths or clothing. We receive an impartation when we capture the *spirit* [128] of the mantle that rests upon a man or woman of God that could take place by association.

The Purpose of the Anointing

In a previous chapter we learned that Jesus taught His disciples about the kingdom in order to help them understand the purpose of power. The same is true with the anointing. We must know what the anointing is in order to use it. Otherwise, it will be worthless to us.

*The Spirit of the LORD is upon me, **for** he has anointed me to bring Good News to the poor. He has sent me to proclaim that captives will be released, that the blind will see, that the oppressed will be set free.* (Luke 4:18 NLT, emphasis added)

The key word in this verse is *"for."* Why did the Holy Spirit descend upon Jesus? Note that each purpose listed is neither selfish nor personally beneficial but rather to *bless* [129] others. We cannot forget that the anointing is given to heal the sick, to cast out demons, to preach the gospel, to perform miracles, and, most important, to exalt Jesus. This is the reason we were separated and consecrated for the ministry. When men and women use their mantles to self-proclaim, self-promote, or gain dishonest earnings to satisfy a personal need for fame and possessions, their end will be painful. There is a sick world out there, full of insecurities, fear, depression, sadness, bitterness, and loneliness. It is a world tormented by wicked spirits; empty, aimless, and in need of someone who is anointed to break strongholds, someone whom God can use to deliver it and give it hope.

It shall come to pass in that day that his burden will be taken away from your shoulder, and his yoke from your neck, and the yoke will be destroyed because of the anointing oil. (Isaiah 10:27)

In my many years of ministry experience, I have observed two different types of anointing, or mantles, operating over certain individuals on earth:

- **Generational Mantles**

Generational mantles are transferred from natural, or spiritual, fathers and mothers to their sons and daughters or when a mentor/disciple relationship is established.

• Special Mantles

These mantles are given by God and placed directly upon certain men to carry out a specific mandate for a particular _generation_ [130]. Once the purpose is carried out, the mantle cannot be duplicated.

---

*A special mantle will often be accompanied by
a small preview of what will come in the future.*

Anointings are being loosened on the earth right now, including some that have never been seen before. Keep your eyes open. We will never wear a new mantle until we let go of the old capes of religion and tradition. If we are not ready to get rid of the old, we will not be ready to receive the new mantle.

> *And David said to Saul, "I cannot walk with these, for I have not tested them." So David took them off.*
> (1 Samuel 17:39)

Saul placed his armor on David before he faced Goliath, but it did not work because it was too heavy, making it impossible for David to move under its weight. Saul's armor symbolized the old, the traditional, and the religious—the old that many of us are used to wearing. Unlike David, who immediately removed the armor, we pretend to walk with the old, even if we hate it and find it uncomfortable.

Sometimes, God allows us to experience a season of feeling burned-out, a season in which nothing happens, in order to help us remove the _old mantle_ [131] and receive a new one. In these cases, we may perceive in our spirits that there is something more, but we have no idea how to receive it. Other times, it causes frustration, desperation, or dissatisfaction to make us seek His face and thereby allow Him to give us the new mantle.

What Are the Consequences of Judging or Refusing a Mantle?

The Word teaches that we will receive a mantle the same way we receive a gift. If we do not respect it—if you criticize it, judge it, or reject it—we will not receive it.

> *He who receives a prophet in the name of a prophet shall receive a prophet's reward.*
> (Matthew 10:41)

The moment someone speaks badly about the mantle or anointing of the man of God, he schedules the funeral for his own mantle. The person who betrays a prophetic mantle will never again flow in the prophetic mantle.

What happened to the apostle Paul? He lived in Corinth for three and a half years. He taught, imparted, and gave his life for the people. Sadly, the people did not grow or mature. They remained as spiritual children. This happened because they did not _receive_ [132] the mantle that God had placed on Paul. However, the same apostle visited the Thessalonians for three weeks, was welcomed there as a man of God, and delivered a message that was accepted as God's Word. As a result, the Thessalonians grew, matured, and evangelized Macedonia.

How many mantles have been rejected by the church? I believe this is a major reason why the body of Christ is incomplete. We cannot live with only one measure, gift, or mantle. We need mantles for healing, miracles, prosperity, worship, wealth, knowledge, politics, government, and so forth. If we did not, God would not have provided these mantles.

What Has Happened to the Fivefold Ministries?

When we reject the pastoral ministry, we fail to care for the sheep, and they are likely to lose their way. If we reject the teacher's mantle, we *parish* [133] for lack of knowledge. (See Hosea 4:6.) When we reject the evangelistic mantle, souls are not saved. When we reject the ministry of the prophet, the church lacks vision and direction concerning the things that God is doing and saying. If we reject the apostolic mantle, the church operates without direction, vision, edification, impartation, revelation, advancement of the kingdom, and supernatural power to perform miracles.

Every time we reject one of the fivefold ministries, the church suffers because God's power cannot fully manifest.

Some mantles have never been used because they were rejected.
The mantle you reject becomes the one that will judge you.

Do not touch My anointed ones, and do My prophets no harm.   (1 Chronicles 16: 22)

In this verse, the word *"touch"* has a negative connotation. It implies *criticism* [134], obstacles, or harm. This indicates that if anybody "touches" the anointed of God, they are, in fact, "touching" God. You cannot touch the anointed without touching the divine mantle that rests upon his or her life.

Consequences of Touching the Mantle

• **Aaron and Miriam touched Moses' mantle.**

Then Miriam and Aaron spoke against Moses because of the Ethiopian woman whom he had married.   (Numbers 12:1)

• **Judgment came upon Miriam.**

"Why then were you not afraid to speak against My servant Moses?"…Suddenly Miriam became leprous, as white as snow.   (Numbers 12:8, 10)

• **Judgment came upon Aaron.**

Take Aaron and Eleazar his son, and bring them up to Mount Hor; and strip Aaron of his garments and put them on Eleazar his son.   (Numbers 20:25–26)

The Main Enemy of the Anointing

The main enemy of the anointing is *familiarity* [135], which may cause us to take lightly, or to disrespect, the mantle upon a man or woman of God. This goes hand in hand with the familiarity people develop toward God's servants and their anointing.

Placing a Demand on the Anointing, or Mantle

To place a demand on a God-given anointing, or mantle, is to express a deep desire or hunger for a supernatural manifestation of God's power. Demand manifests by faith. For example, when a pastor is preaching and he suddenly stops to call someone with a specific condition to come forward for prayer, deliverance, or healing, it is because a demand had been made. Some preachers struggle to minister and teach because of familiarity and conformity. When people conform, they no longer exert the same level of demand upon the anointing of a man or woman of God. As a result, the power of God fails to manifest within them. Familiarity produces conformity and disrespect with the result being that people become unable to receive from that mantle.

If a person cannot receive from my mantle,
it means that he is not ready to receive it.

How Do Faith and the Anointing Work Together?

The anointing is never received by skeptics, only by people who exercise their faith. People absorb the gift in the mantle, and, in the end, the preacher does not need to minister to these people, as they have already received through the Word.

When a person does not place a demand on the anointing,
he or she stops being a recipient of the anointing.

Faith can keep a man preaching even when he does not want to continue. This is not always understood, but it is caused by someone placing a *demand*[136] and not letting go until something happens.

Individual faith can powerfully influence the anointing on a man of God.

How Do We Receive the Benefits of a Mantle?

I have asked the Lord what needs to be done for my anointing to flow through my spiritual children. Then, I notice that some were already flowing in the fullness of my mantle, some only had a portion of it, and others barely had it. It was then that the Lord taught me four principles about receiving the benefits of the mantle or the anointing:

It is like the precious oil upon the head, running down on the beard, the beard of Aaron,
running down on the edge of his garments. (Psalm 133:2)

1. Recognize the mantle.

To recognize the mantle is to realize that the leader is the person God has chosen as an authority over our life. This is the person who will take us to our *inheritance*[137]—the one whom we must submit to and obey. That man or woman is the vessel God will use to pour the anointing into our life and loosen our purposes and destinies. He or she will also lead us to flow in the same level of his or her anointing.

2. Receive the mantle.

We must welcome this person as the anointed one of God and understand that his or her message is the living Word of God. It is also important to understand that anointed men and women have weaknesses as well as strengths. Therefore, we cannot expect that person to be perfect *before* welcoming him or her.

You cannot receive the strengths of the anointed
if you do not accept their weaknesses.

---

3. Honor the mantle.

Honor is demonstrated verbally and materially through __*obedience*__ (138) and submission. In the Old Testament, no one could approach a man of God with empty hands, not because the anointing could be purchased but because it was a matter of honor. The Bible demonstrates the power of honor when God affirms that if we give a glass of water to a prophet, we will have the prophet's reward. (See Matthew 10:41–42.)

Honor gives us access to the reward system of a man or woman of God.

---

4. Serve the mantle.

Serving the mantle implies working and sowing into the mantle without a personal agenda. It means loving the man of God and the mantle that God has deposited upon him. The Lord once said to me, "When your disciples and spiritual children obey these principles, they will flow under your same anointing.".

You are able only to carry the mantle of the one you serve.

What Signs Indicate That God Has Loosened a New Mantle?

- God gives hunger and thirst that cannot be __*satiated*__ (139), and those who experience them place a demand on the mantle. If God were to cut off the flow of the anointing, I would end up doing courtesy prayers.

- God changes our spiritual appetites. We no longer want the spiritual milk of the Word, but we seek to satisfy our hunger with meat and vegetables. We want messages that help us grow, mature, and become disciplined so that we can commit to God's service and seek more of Him.

- God gives us a strong desire to change. Regardless of age, if you are ready for change, God will give you a new mantle and impartation.

How Are the Mantle and Impartation Given?

• God loosens the mantle directly upon a man.

In most cases, the man receives a revelation—a mandate from God or a supernatural _visitation_ (140)—as it happened to Jesus and others.

• A man transfers his mantle to another.

This can happen three ways: by atmosphere, by association, or by influence.

Your blessings and destiny are closely related with those to whom God has connected you.

This is the reason divine relationships are heavily attacked by the devil. When God connects us to someone, Satan will do anything he can to destroy that relationship because he knows that if we never make such a connection, our purpose will never be carried out and completed. God will connect us to other people. Therefore, we must become wise discerners of relationships.

The anointing you receive by association can be lost if you begin to criticize or dishonor the mantle you have received.

What Must Happen for God to Give Us a Mantle?

1. We must hunger for, thirst for, and desire it.

Those who _genuinely_ (141) desire the anointing are the best candidates for receiving it. In the natural, if we feel the hunger for it, we will tend to forget the norms of courtesy because we seek only to satisfy our yearnings The same happens in the spirit realm. Only those who hunger and thirst for the anointing are candidates to receive a mantle and the anointing.

Without this awareness, he will not seek the anointing with passion or risk anything to acquire it. However, in some instances, as time passes, that passion for the anointing begins to subside, and we stop being aware of the need for it in our lives.

2. We must be prepared to pay the price.

The belief that the anointing is free is a great misconception.

Countless preachers have cheapened the anointing. Consequently, today's youth regard the pastoral office as one more career choice instead of a holy ministerial calling.

Why Lay Hands on Someone When Transferring a Mantle?

• To activate

• To _impart_ (142)

• To identify

I cannot activate something in you if you are not willing to do God's will. I cannot impart the anointing over you if you do not resolve to use it to bless others. Likewise, I will not lay hands on you if you do not identify with the anointing that is on me. We are activating too many people who are rebellious by nature. Therefore, it is important for the pastor to carefully choose a leadership team he can activate with his mantle and impartation.

3. The anointing, or mantle, must be planted, not thrown away.

Fatherhood and discipleship are sown by continually teaching, training, and equipping the people. If a seed is simply thrown to the ground, it is wasted, but if it is planted, it grows and bears fruit. When the mantle, or the anointing, is planted or sown, people begin to flow in the same mantle because that is what they received. As the mentor/disciple or father/son relationship grows, the flow of the mantle and its manifestation also grows. This is indicative that the mantle also is growing.

We will flow in the same anointing as the mantle we serve.

---

4. The mantle must be cultivated.

For the anointing to *increase* (143.), we must cultivate our mantle. This will keep us permanently connected to the source of the mantle. If we fail to do this, the anointing will weaken.

5. We must develop covenantal relationships.

God will cause our relationships to change because one key to becoming carriers of the anointing is not to be emotionally tied to people who are potential obstacles to us receiving and flowing in a new anointing, especially if those people have a traditional, denominational, and rigid mentality that keeps them from changing for the better.

In conclusion, it is important to discern the present move of God. There are waves and moves of the Holy Spirit we cannot afford to overlook, or we will be left behind only to realize later that God is no longer where we expect to find Him.

The church needs to constantly seek divine revelation. Its survival will be determined by the degree of preparation it undertakes in order to walk in the supernatural. God is raising a new generation of people who know how to walk in the dimension of eternity and know how to draw forth the wealth of the spiritual world.

7

Glory: The Third Dimension of the Supernatural

I have written this chapter to aid you in the transition from the anointing into God's glory and to awaken this present generation to the benefits of moving into, and permanently remaining within, the presence of God.

Glory, in the Beginning

And the Lord God formed man of the dust of the ground, and breathed into his nostrils the breath of life; and man became a living being. (Genesis 2:7)

In the beginning, God created man in His image and likeness, shaping him from the dust of the earth and breathing into him the breath of life. That breath was God's *glory* [144]. At that moment, God imparted the fullness of His virtues, nature, and glory to man. In that realm, the mind of man functioned at 100 percent because the mind of the Spirit was in him to exercise dominion and lordship over creation. Within God's glory, mankind had no understanding of sickness, death, poverty, depression, or sadness because his original design did not recognize these trials. He did not have to wait to gather the harvest because waiting implies a space in time, and glory is eternity where everything is now. Plants and trees grew as each seed hit the ground. The Word teaches that when creation took place, everything was already fruitful and mature. Even Adam was spared the stages of growth that we must endure. It is important to stop here for a moment and note that Jesus did experience each stage of growth, and this is why He has the ability to comprehend what it feels like to be a child, a teenager, and an adult. He understands what it feels like to be rejected, judged, and condemned. But these experiences were unknown to Adam before the fall. In the dimension of glory, earth was completely fertile. Its order was harvest/seed rather than seed/harvest. What happened after Adam sinned?

For all have sinned and fall short of the glory of God. (Romans 3:23)

I believe that when God went looking for Adam and Eve in the garden, instead of spending time with them, He cursed the earth and *withdrew* [145] His presence. In fact, I believe that He then inhaled His glory from Adam's body. At that moment, man exited the dimension of glory and began to experience death, though not immediately. As an added note of interest, we could say that the residue of glory that lingered in Adam was enough for him to live to the age of nine hundred thirty years. That inheritance was passed down to future generations, and they also enjoyed years of life into the hundreds.

Everything that has God's glory has life. Death indicates an absence of His glory.

When Adam sinned, something shifted in the mind of man. Many lines of genuine knowledge were disconnected from its original source, and the human brain lost a major percentage of usage. Today, scientists have discovered that we use only a ten percent of our cerebral capacity, which could lead to the conclusion that Adam substituted limited rational knowledge for infinite revealed knowledge. In the case of Albert Einstein, whose ability to reason well exceeded that of the average human, he used a little more brain capacity than an average man. If the average man, despite his limitations, has been able to make so many discoveries, travel into space, and develop cures to countless sicknesses, among other achievements, imagine how spectacular Adam's mind must have been under God's glory. This is why we must recover our mental capacity. It is also what the Bible refers to when it urges us to renew our minds.

After Adam's fall, God cursed the land, and man was _disconnected_ (146) from His glory. Thus, the process of provision is no longer harvest/seed, as it was in the beginning, but seed/time/harvest.

> *While the earth remains, seedtime and harvest, cold and heat, winter and summer, and day and night shall not cease.*   (Genesis 8:22)

Today, we go from process to process, each process taking time to complete. As a result of the curse, which has left us dependent on time, we must wait to gather the harvest or reach a goal. This is precisely why God gave us faith—to break the law of time. When His presence manifests itself, everything in the natural accelerates, and the supernatural appears.

> *"Behold, the days are coming," says the LORD, "When the plowman shall overtake the reaper, and the treader of grapes him who sows seed."*   (Amos 9:13)

The key word in this verse is *"overtake."* God promises to loosen the house, the job, or anything else we need, as long as we believe we will receive it. I have seen God cancel debt instantaneously. This is one good reason for us to stay full of faith. Our seed will activate the promise of God to accelerate His provision.

Now that we understand what happened after Adam sinned, let's understand the revelation of glory.

What Is the Glory of God?

The Hebrew for "glory" is *kabowd*, which means "glory, honor, glorious, abundance." It comes from a root word meaning "to be heavy, be weighty...rich." *Kabowd* is used in describing wealthy men of great reputation, but it is also used to refer to God. In Greek, the word used for "glory" is *doxa*, meaning "splendor, brightness...magnificence, excellence, preeminence, dignity, grace." In essence, this word gives us the fundamental meaning of who God is—His attributes, virtues, character, nature, and perfection. God's glory is the intrinsic _essence_ (147) of His presence.

As we discuss the glory of God, it is also important to note that there exists the glory of men and the glory of the world. The Bible describes these types of glory as vain and temporal, consisting only of prestige, fame, position, comfort, reputation, and recognition.

The lust of the flesh, the lust of the eyes, and the pride of life; is not of the Father but is of the world. (1 John 2:16)

The Word also mentions the glory of terrestrial and celestial bodies. It teaches that the external glory reflected by a body shows the internal condition of the same. This external glory is the intrinsic value and worth of the body.

There are also celestial bodies and terrestrial bodies; but the glory of the celestial is one, and the glory of the terrestrial is another. (1 Corinthians 15:40)

God's glory is the _visible_ [148] and tangible manifestation of the fullness of His presence impacting the physical senses. It is God making Himself tangible. In the Old Testament, God manifested in the form of a cloud known as *shekinah*, which means "dwelling, settling." It refers to the dwelling or settling presence of God among His people, as well as the eminent, transcending presence of God. God manifests Himself in the physical realm. In other words, He goes from the spiritual realm into the natural realm. *Shekinah* comes from the root word *shakan*, "to settle down, abide, dwell, tabernacle, reside." God's will and desire have always included dwelling, resting, and living among His people.

God's glory is the manifested presence of Yahweh.

• God appeared to Abraham.

The God of glory appeared to our father Abraham when he was in Mesopotamia, before he dwelt in Haran. (Acts 7:2)

The physical manifestation of God's glory transformed Abraham forever, changing his life, motives, priorities, and intentions.

• God manifested His glory to the Israelite nation.

So it was always: the cloud covered it by day, and the appearance of fire by night. (Numbers 9:16)

God manifested His glory to the Israelites in the form of a pillar of _cloud_ [149] and a pillar of fire. The cloud protected the people from the sweltering heat of the desert during the day, and the fire kept them warm at night, when the temperatures dipped to near freezing. Under the protective covering of that glory—*shekinah*—many supernatural events took place: the Red Sea opened before them, manna descended from heaven, and their footwear never wore out. During the forty years they walked the desert, no one experienced sickness, and God provided water from a rock and kept the giants from destroying them. These are only a few of the supernatural events that took place.

• God revealed His glory through Christ.

And the Word became flesh and dwelt among us, and we beheld His glory, the glory as of the only begotten of the Father, full of grace and truth. (John 1:14)

Jesus came to reveal the Father's glory—the glory that was lost by Adam. Through His death and resurrection, Jesus led us back to that dimension of glory.

...bringing many sons to glory. (Hebrews 2:10)

Jesus endured our shame so we could share in His glory.

Everything the Father is—His virtues, attributes, character, nature, power, authority, and grace—was manifested in His Son. Furthermore, Jesus promised to manifest Himself to those who ___obeyed___ [150] His Word.

Just before His arrest, Jesus prayed to the Father, asking Him to return the glory that mankind had lost so that each believer could live in its manifestation.

> *As You sent Me into the world, I also have sent them into the world. And for their sakes I sanctify Myself, that they also may be sanctified by the truth....And the glory which You gave Me I have given them, that they may be one just as We are one....that they may behold My glory which You have given Me.* (John 17:18–19, 22, 24)

How Do We Enter Into the Manifestation of God's Glory?

Holy, holy, holy is the LORD of hosts; the whole earth is full of His glory! (Isaiah 6:3)

Scripture affirms that the earth is full of God's glory, but the channel—or tool—that grants access to the manifestation of glory in the natural realm is revelation, not reason. While it is true that God's presence is everywhere, it is also true that He does not manifest everywhere.

God created the heavens and the earth and filled them with His glory. However, I want to highlight Genesis 1, which informs us that before God initiated the process of creation, He sent His Holy Spirit to set up camp with His energy—His glory—in order to make ___creation___ [151] possible.

> *And the Spirit of God was hovering over the face of the waters.* (Genesis 1:2)

When God plans to do something, He first sends His Holy Spirit, followed by His Word.

Paul made reference to God's energy, His glory, and affirmed the following:

> *To this end I also labor, striving according to His working [energeia] which works [energeo] in me mightily.* (Colossians 1:29)

The literal translation of this verse suggests that Paul worked hard and gave his best because of the energy, or power, God gave him. This energy activated a miraculous power within Paul that elevated his capacity, potential, and authority.

God's glory provides the necessary energy to create any matter.

God's glory has been upon the earth since creation. Ever since the fall of man, however, we have been unable to see or work with it. But if His glory exists on the earth with the power of creation, then God can create a new heart, lung, ear, eye, arm, or any other organ that is missing. But this happens only when the Holy Spirit moves and God acts on His Word. The key, therefore, is _knowing_ [152] how to call forth a visible manifestation of God's glory in the natural realm.

God's glory makes no sense without revealed knowledge.

What Is Revealed Knowledge?

For the earth will be filled with the knowledge of the glory of the LORD, as the waters cover the sea.   (Habakkuk 2:14)

The word *"knowledge"*, as used in this verse, is the Hebrew word *yada,* meaning "to know, learn to know…to perceive and see, find out and discern…to discriminate, distinguish…to know, be acquainted with." It is also used in Genesis 4:1 to describe sexual intimacy between Adam and Eve.

In Greek, this word is translated as *gnosis* or *epignosis.* The former is scientific or theoretic knowledge, and the latter refers to observable, practical knowledge. *Epignosis* means "precise and correct knowledge." Revealed knowledge comes to our spirits when we have a close, intimate relationship with God.

Knowledge will never become ours until we obey it, practice it, and experience it.

God's glory is _initiated_ [153] only by God and for God, not by man. Therefore, there is formula or pattern that can be followed in order to activate and flow in His glory. I believe that our generation will see the former glory (the miracles of the Old Testament) and latter glory (the miracles Jesus predicted would occur in the church) manifesting together. God is raising apostles and prophets to bring this revelation to our generation. He is opening the heavens and pouring out the revelation we need to manifest His glory. For centuries, the church has been seeking manifestations of power without success, not because God has chosen not to manifest but because the church lacks the required faith and knowledge to manifest His glory.

A revelation from God will undoubtedly lead you to a supernatural experience.

If ever there was a time for God to deliver the revealed knowledge of His glory, I believe it is now. Many prophets, including Isaiah, Habakkuk, and Haggai, prophesied of the glory but never fully experienced it. They died with their hopes rooted in this era, which leads us to deduce that we are living in the final move of God, in which the earth will be full of His knowledge and glory. Then, we will experience the greatest _manifestations_ [154] ever seen in history, and no man will be able to attribute that glory to himself.

If a person never receives revelation, he will not see continuous manifestations.

The mistake many people make is that they move in the glory for a short time and later return to the anointing because they failed to allow God to take the initiative. Thus, they learned to operate by faith under the anointing, but they never learned to move in the glory because it is an unknown dimension in which the initiative belongs to God. Glory demands a greater degree of humility and dependence on God. It demands pure motives and audacity in the Holy Spirit.

God will not visit us with His glory beyond the revelation we have of it.

If the Lord visits us with His glory and we are not ready for it, it can kill us. If He brings forth unusual manifestations, creative miracles, signs, and wonders, but we lack the revelation to receive them, we will judge and criticize what is happening, thereby grieving the Holy Spirit. When the manifestation of God's glory comes, we must know how to deal with it.

The glory we preach can also kill us.

How Do Glory, Faith, and the Anointing Operate?

Faith is the ability given to the believer by God to have dominion over time, space, and matter. Anointing is the ability given to the believer by God to do whatever He has called him or her to do. It is Jesus working through humanity. Glory is the presence of God manifested in visible form. It is God doing His *works* (155) and operating according to His sovereignty and initiative.

Now, let us see how faith, the anointing, and glory operate.

• **Faith operates in dimensions.**

As we established earlier, *"from faith to faith."* This means we are able to go from one dimension of faith to another dimension of faith.

For in [the gospel] *the righteousness of God is revealed from faith to faith.*

(Romans 1:17)

• **The anointing operates in levels.**

The apostle Paul, according to the original text written in Greek, affirmed the following:

But we all...are being transformed into the same image from glory to glory.

(2 Corinthians 3:18)

There are many levels of the anointing. With spiritual *gifts* (156), we can minister to one or several members of the body of Christ. With the anointing, we can reach *multitudes*.(157)

• **The glory operates in dimensions.**

With the glory, we can reach and impact nations. If something took ten years to accomplish under the anointing, we will be able to do it in one year under the glory.

The Manifested Glory—the Presence of God—
Operates on the Basis of:

• God's sovereignty

This means that God does what He wants, when He wants, and how He wants. We must allow the Holy Spirit to manifest the sovereignty of God and allow Him to do as He wills.

Do not be hasty to go from his presence. Do not take your stand for an evil thing, for he does whatever pleases him.   (Ecclesiastes 8:3)

• God's initiative

Jesus is the Head of the church. Therefore, He must initiate the action and move as He wants. However, there are times when God does not initiate the action because He has already told us in His Word what to do. When this happens, it is best to do what He has *commanded*[158] us to do, making sure that we understand His command and do not invent something just to get it over and done with. Let us not confuse this with what King Saul did—he waited for the prophet Samuel to offer the sacrifice unto the Lord, but, since the prophet delayed, he decided to do it himself—which he was not permitted to do. (See 1 Samuel 13:6–14.) Do you see the difference?

Most believers understand the concept of God's sovereignty, but what they don't understand is how to live in it by faith.

• Always waiting for God to take the initiative

On occasions when God's presence has not yet manifested, we must then exercise our faith, anointing, and gifts. If we do nothing, *always* waiting for God to take the initiative, then we are working in the extreme.

• Always taking the initiative from the human point of view

This refers to churches that are conducted entirely by man-made plans, which lead only to doing works that are void of God's power and presence.

8

Miracles, Signs, Wonders, and Casting Out Demons

Jesus has not changed. He is the same yesterday, today, and forever. (See Hebrews 13:8.) His conception and birth through a young virgin was a miracle. His knowledge and wisdom, which confused the erudite experts in the law, were miracles. His entire ministry was a torrent of miracles that inspired awe and wonder in the multitudes that witnessed them. Even His conviction and death sentence were miracles, as He was completely innocent of the charges. His crucifixion, death, and resurrection were also miraculous events. As its name implies, the book of Acts is filled with the many miracles, signs, and wonders performed by the disciples of Jesus. In almost every chapter, there are descriptions of supernatural "acts" that took place after the Holy Spirit descended upon the faithful. Through them, the early church was able to proclaim His name with power and supernatural evidence. Today, we have the same privilege.

Jesus *delegated* (159) His ministry of miracles to the church, which angered the Jewish leaders of His time. When miracles are absent from Christianity, there is nothing new to offer an unbelieving world other than another form of religion with the appearance of godliness.

Christianity is life—the nature of Jesus manifested through His people. In the Old Testament, the purpose of miracles was to divert people's attention from their worship of pagan gods and to lead them in worship of the only true God. In those days, when miracles ceased, people quickly reverted to their old rituals and pagan ceremonies. The same thing is happening today. Most churches are full of people who need a miracle from God today, because, tomorrow, they will look for it somewhere else.

My Experience with Jesus, the Miracle-Working God

I have enjoyed many incredible personal experiences with my beloved Jesus:

- I have seen Jesus perform miracles, signs, and wonders in His Word.

- I have personally witnessed the real, resurrected Christ performing miracles, signs, and wonders through men and women, both in the past and the present time.

- I have personally experienced, and continue to experience, being used by God to perform miracles, signs, and wonders.

- I work to teach, train, and equip others to be used by God in ministries of miracles.

I have witnessed the blind see, the deaf-mute hear and speak, and the lame walk. I have seen people suffering from cancer, AIDS, and other supposedly incurable diseases walk away completely healed. I have seen flesh and bone created where there were none before. I have witnessed wonderfully unusual miracles, such as the growth of new teeth, the appearance of hair on bald heads, and the loss of weight in mere seconds. All of these miracles were done in the powerful name of Jesus. No longer must we go back to the days of the apostles to read of miracles. We can see them with our own eyes. Jesus was raised from the dead, He is alive, and He continues to perform miracles today.

The only way to know that Jesus lives is to see Him perform the same miracles He did while He walked on earth.

One problem with _religion_ [160] today is its inability to bring Jesus into the present. It focuses on the past and future but they ignore the present. If Jesus is unable to do miracles today, why call Him God? If God cannot perform miracles, how can we refer to Him as being love?

Genuine faith brings Jesus into the now.

In order to understand a few facts about the supernatural, let's define a few fundamental terms. Furthermore, let's examine the difference between them.

What Is Healing?

In the Greek text of the New Testament, there are several words used to describe healing, although I will touch on only the three that are used most often. The first is *iasis*, which means "a healing, cure." It generally refers to an act of healing, such as:

> *Behold, I cast out demons and perform cures [iasis] today and tomorrow, and the third day I shall be perfected.* (Luke 13:32)

The second word, *therapeia*, means a "service rendered by one to another...a specific medical service: curing, healing."

> *They followed Him; and He received them and spoke to them about the kingdom of God, and healed those who had need of healing [therapeia].* (Luke 9:11)

The third word, *iaomai*, is a much more complex term because, in addition to being defined as "a means of healing, remedy, medicine," it also means "to make whole...to free from errors and sins, to bring about (one's) salvation." This was the _ministry_ [161] of Jesus.

> *God anointed Jesus of Nazareth with the Holy Spirit and with power, who went about doing good and healing [iaomai] all who were oppressed by the devil, for God was with Him.* (Acts 10:38)

> *They will lay hands on the sick, and they will recover.* (Mark 16:18)

I know many believers who personally understand what Paul meant when he confessed that he had a thorn in his flesh. (See 2 Corinthians 12:7.) I know of those who have experienced

Job's boils (see Job 2:7), Timothy's stomach pain (see 1 Timothy 5:23), and much more. Some take comfort in their malady, thinking that the sickness is a punishment sent by God, or that their suffering brings glory to God. Others use the Bible to try to justify their illnesses. None of these things is scripturally correct. Few of them can quote verses on healing because pastors have failed to teach on the subject.

According to Scripture, the power of sickness was destroyed by Christ over two thousand years ago. If this is so, why are people still getting sick? In truth, sickness expired the day Jesus paid the price for our iniquities on the cross of Calvary. Therefore, it is _illegal_ (162) for sickness to enter the bodies of believers. Healing is not a divine gift; it is a legal right. Yet the church continues to seek the "gift" of healing more than the "right" of healing.

> *Healing is a legal right that belongs to the believer, for his or her life,*
> *and to impart into the lives of others.*

What Is a Miracle?

As I mentioned earlier, the Greek word for "miracle" is *dynamis*, which means "strength power, ability...inherent power, power residing in a thing by virtue of its nature." Miracles, therefore, manifest God's supernatural power. They are God's visible, spontaneous, and sudden intervention into the normal course of an individual's life, an interruption of the natural laws of time, space, and matter.

> *Truly the signs of an apostle were accomplished among you with all perseverance, in*
> *signs and wonders and mighty deeds.* (2 Corinthians 12:12)

What Is the Difference Between a Healing and a Miracle?

A miracle is an _instantaneous_ (163) event that is evident to the human senses, while healing is _progressive_ (164). So, a miracle produces a change that goes beyond healing. The call for a miracle is not a sign of ignorance or weakness but an intense desire to touch the invisible God and to see Him in action.

> *A miracle performed in the name of Jesus is more valuable*
> *than a year of academic theory.*

What Is a Sign?

The word "sign" comes from the Greek word *semeion*, which means "a sign, mark, token...miracles and wonders by which God authenticates the men sent by him." A sign is a _demonstration_ (165) of God's love or a seal that signifies that person is distinguished or acknowledged. *Semeion* refers to a wondrous occurrence that takes place in an unusual way and transcends the common course of the natural world. God uses signs to authenticate those He sends, as well as to prove that the cause he or she is defending also comes from Him. The signs of God are used not only to help people but also to give glory to His Son, Jesus.

God performs signs as allegories to communicate a great truth of the kingdom and of Jesus.

We must pay close attention because there is a great difference between recognizing the signs that follow us and worshipping those signs. God prohibits our _worship_ [166] of signs. Yes, signs will follow those He sends, but only when their passion for God goes beyond their passion for the appearance of signs.

Seven Signs That Prove the Deity of Jesus

This beginning of signs Jesus did in Cana of Galilee, and manifested His glory; and His disciples believed in Him.   (John 2:11)

The gospel of John is structured around seven miraculous signs performed by Jesus in order to demonstrate and prove His deity. Each sign has its own profound meaning.

1. At a wedding in Cana, Jesus turned the water into wine. (See John 2:1–11.) It marked the transition of the believer from the old wine to the new wine.

2. Jesus healed the nobleman's son in Capernaum. (See John 4:46–54.) This sign showed the importance of believing in God by faith in the authority of His Word rather than relying only on His works.

3. Jesus healed the man at the pool of Bethesda. (See John 5:1–15.) This sign symbolized the need for people to leave behind the wounds of their past and to move forward.

4. Jesus fed five thousand people with five loaves and two small fish. (See John 6:1–13.) This was a metaphor of becoming a channel for God to multiply and spiritually feed the multitudes.

5. Jesus walked on water. (See John 6:16–21.) This marked Jesus' authority over the elements of nature.

6. Jesus healed a man blind from birth by covering his eyes with mud. (See John 9:1–7.) This illustrated religious blindness and of the Pharisaic mentality. It also demonstrated how the Son of God restored spiritual vision.

7. Jesus raised Lazarus from the dead. (See John 11:1–45.) This symbolized that Jesus is the resurrection and the life, and that He exercises dominion over death.

The purpose of these signs was to _prove_ [167] that Jesus was the Messiah—the Son of God—and that He was capable of giving them eternal life, along with the ability to see, hear, and experience an intimate communion with God the Father. Each sign pointed not to a man, a temple, or an organization, but only to Jesus.

What Are Wonders?

The Greek word for "wonder" is *teras*, meaning "a prodigy, portent...miracle: performed by anyone." It describes something unusual that dazzles and amazes the spectator, and its origin can be described only as a sign from heaven—a divine act.

Then fear came upon every soul, and many wonders and signs were done through the apostles.
(Acts 2:43)

The difference between a sign and wonder is that a sign points to something or someone specific—for example, Jesus—while a wonder appeals to the imagination, the intellect, and the heart of the observer, amazing him and leading him to receive the gospel.

What Is the Casting Out of Demons?

The war between the kingdom of God and the kingdom of darkness is fought over the dominion of the human *soul* [168]. God created us, but Satan has worked hard to destroy us because he hates God and anything that resembles Him. Satan pretends to govern the earth in order to gain lordship over the Father's most valuable possession: His children—us! When an individual refuses to welcome Jesus into his heart, the enemy takes over that place and colonizes the territory, blinding that individual and preventing him from seeing and knowing the Son of God. Satan's ultimate goal is to contaminate mankind with sin, sickness, and death, and to eternally separate us from the Father. But Jesus came to stop him and his evil works.

Two kingdoms cannot govern an individual. The casting out of demons implies the establishment of the kingdom of light with the subsequent displacement of the kingdom of darkness. Jesus came to establish the kingdom of heaven on earth. He has the power to cast Satan out. Jesus went to hell and took the keys of death and Hades away from the devil. (See Revelation 1:18.) Then, He gave us the authority, in His name, to do the same. (See Luke 10:19.)

Thus, the casting out of demons is the act of *uprooting* [169] them from a body they control on the basis of Jesus' delegated authority and the power of the Holy Spirit. In other words, to cast out a demon is to dethrone Satan and stop his control of an individual, thereby allowing the light of Jesus to shine on that person and lead him to reconciliation with the Father. This process makes the person an active member of the kingdom of heaven, taking him from death to life.

*Now John answered Him, saying, "Teacher, we saw someone who does not follow us **casting out demons** in Your name, and we forbade him because he does not follow us." But Jesus said, "Do not forbid him, for no one who works **a miracle** in My name can soon afterward speak evil of Me."*
(Mark 9:38–39, emphasis added)

In the verse above, we see a direct relationship between miracles and the casting out of demons. The casting out of demons is a miracle because it is a supernatural occurrence.

And the multitudes with one accord heeded the things spoken by Philip, hearing and seeing the miracles which he did. For unclean spirits, crying with a loud voice, came out of many who were possessed; and many who were paralyzed and lame were healed.
(Acts 8:6–7)

The signs mentioned in these verses were visible miracles that happened instantaneously, before the eyes of witnesses. In my years of ministry, as I have ministered the supernatural power of God, I have discovered that many illnesses are related to _demonic_ [170] activity in the body, emotions, and/or bloodline. When we cast out demons from people, frequently, they are healed instantly.

The casting out of demons is a visible manifestation of the presence of the kingdom of God.

Now God worked unusual miracles by the hands of Paul. (Acts 19:11)

For the members of the early church, miracles were an everyday, normal occurrence. Every miracle performed by God is amazing and wonderful, but some seem to have a more dramatic effect than others.

Healing, miracles, signs, wonders, and the casting out of demons are keys to expanding God's kingdom on earth.

People who personally experience a miracle exercise their faith. They do not idly stand by, waiting for something to happen. It is important to clarify that Jesus performed miracles through many different means. The Holy Spirit does not always do things the same way. Sometimes, Jesus barely touched the person. Other times, He laid hands on him or her. In other cases, He declared the Word, touched the person's ear, or made mud with His saliva. If we desire the supernatural, we must be _flexible_ [171] and ready to obey the Holy Spirit at a moment's notice.

Ways God Confirmed and Validated the Ministry of Jesus

• With miracles, signs, wonders, and the gifts of the Holy Spirit

God also bearing witness both with signs and wonders, with various miracles, and gifts of the Holy Spirit, according to His own will.... (Hebrews 2:4)

God testified to Jesus with four methods: miracles, signs, wonders, and the gifts of the Holy Spirit. It is important to keep in mind that, because of their culture, the Jews required signs from men who claimed to be of God. They did not acknowledge anyone as a prophet until they saw some demonstration of supernatural signs. Thus, every prophet in the Old Testament distinguished his ministry with signs and miracles. We will never reach the Jews—much less the Muslim nations—with a gospel that lacks supernatural signs and wonders.

This man came to Jesus by night and said to Him, "Rabbi, we know that You are a teacher come from God; for no one can do these signs that You do unless God is with him." (John 3:2)

No man moves in the supernatural if a truth does not exceed the common.

In the history of the church, everyone who has ever moved in miracles, signs, and wonders was obeying a revelation of God, which was *confirmed* [172] by His Word. These men and women left their legacies on earth. They were pioneers who went ahead of their generation in order to teach its members to do the same, and to transfer their legacies to the future generations.

In the twentieth century, God has raised, and continues to raise, men and women with revelation. Their names are immediately associated with the power in which they operate. For instance, when I mention Pastor William Seymour, I think of revival and miracles. When I bring up A. A. Allen, I see miracles and saved souls. The same goes for Yiye Ávila. When I think of Carlos Annacondia, I think of salvation and deliverance. Omar Cabrera personifies salvation and the destruction of strongholds. Bill Hamon deals with the prophetic word, Alan Vincent with the revelation of the kingdom and spiritual warfare, Dr. T. L. Osborn with miracles, healing, prodigies, and salvation, and Morris Cerullo with miracles, salvation, and the prophetic move of the Spirit. Likewise, when I think of Apostle Cash Luna, I associate him with healing, miracles, and finances.

- **By approving the ministry of His Son**

Men of Israel, hear these words: Jesus of Nazareth, a Man attested by God to you by miracles, wonders, and signs which God did through Him in your midst, as you yourselves also know.
(Acts 2:22)

God approves and *validates* [173] our ministries the same way He approved the ministry of His Son—with miracles, signs, and wonders.

- **By confirming His identity as the Messiah**

Jesus answered and said to them, "Go and tell John the things which you hear and see: the blind see and the lame walk; the lepers are cleansed and the deaf hear; the dead are raised up and the poor have the gospel preached to them." (Matthew 11:4–5)

These verses constitute the reply of Jesus to John the Baptist, who, after declaring Jesus to be the Messiah and the Lamb of God, who takes away the sin of the world (see John 1:29), doubted the truth after he was imprisoned. The thing to admire here is that Jesus did not answer by recounting His many personal achievements or by telling John how good or holy He was. Rather, He reminded John's messenger of all the supernatural works God was doing through Him, and how this confirmed His identity as the true Messiah. These should be our credentials, as well.

What Purpose Is There in Miracles, Signs, and Wonders?

Certainly, there has been excesses and abuse in the area of miracles. This, however, should not be an obstacle to manifesting them, because those who have feared the excesses have ended up on the other extreme: living without God's power or miracles. To shed light on this matter, let us examine the biblical purpose for miracles.

- **Miracles *testify* [174] that Jesus is the Son of God.**

If I do not do the works of My Father, do not believe Me; but if I do, though you do not believe Me, believe the works, that you may know and believe that the Father is in Me, and I in Him. (John 10:37–38)

We live in a generation that yearns to see the power of Jesus. Many motivational preachers deliver inspirational messages that simply meet the temporal need of the people, but they are unable to prove with supernatural evidence that Jesus is the Son of God. It is an insult to the cross to preach a message that does not deliver.

- **Miracles speak an allegoric truth concerning the kingdom of God.**

So He took the blind man by the hand and led him out of the town. And when He had spit on his eyes and put His hands on him, He asked him if he saw anything.

(Mark 8:23)

Every time Jesus performed a miracle, it was to illustrate the spiritual condition of the people to confirm His identity as the Son of God. For instance, when He healed the blind, He illustrated spiritual blindness.

- **Miracles *persuade* (175) people who thirst for God to seek Him.**

Some people want to perform miracles but feel they will not be able to until they develop better character. This is a traditional religious mentality because the Bible does not mention the need to have a developed character before moving in miracles. Although I consider character to be essential for living a holy life, it is not essential to perform miracles. All that is needed for miracles to happen is to do them in the name of Jesus. Sadly, some people are desperately seeking God without success. For them, a miracle is the sign that can show them where to find the God they desperately yearn for.

- **Miracles, signs, and wonders expand and establish the kingdom in hostile territories.**

For our gospel did not come to you in word only, but also in power, and in the Holy Spirit and in much assurance. (1 Thessalonians 1:5)

A few years ago, Miami was referred to as a "cemetery" for pastors because it was a difficult place for churches to grow and develop. For almost a generation—over forty years—churches were unable to grow beyond twenty-five hundred members. However, when we started to preach the gospel of the kingdom with *demonstrations* (176) of God's power, including miracles, signs, and wonders, the city opened up. We became the fastest-growing Hispanic church in the United States, and, today, we continue to grow. We are one of the pioneering churches of Miami, and God has raised other anointed men to serve Him in other sectors of the city. At first, there was great opposition from several pastors who were not in agreement with the subject of deliverance and miracles, but God quickly testified of our veracity and confirmed that He had sent us. Many of those pastors today send men and women to our Leadership Institute to be trained and equipped to serve as leaders in their churches.

- **Miracles, signs, and wonders plant churches that grow and stand firm.**

We find this pattern in Scripture: wherever a church or ministry was planted on the foundation of the supernatural—miracles, signs, and wonders—there was rapid growth that naturally affected the entire region. In my experience with planting churches and helping others to do the same, I have observed that the keys to acceleration are evangelism, prayer, deliverance, the restoration of the family, miracles, signs, and wonders.

- **Miracles, signs, and wonders evangelize throughout the world.**

And this gospel of the kingdom will be preached in all the world as a witness to all the nations, and then the end will come. (Matthew 24:14)

To testify is to make something *evident* (177). This verse says, in other words, "This gospel will be proclaimed to make evident and manifest God's supernatural power to all the nations of the world." It will be a replica of the ministry of Jesus. Otherwise, it is not the gospel of the kingdom.

- **Miracles, signs, and wonders challenge the minds of skeptics and others who are hostile toward the gospel.**

When God manifests miracles, signs, and wonders, people are amazed and convicted. This is one way people are encouraged to change their ways and respond to the gospel.

- **Miracles, signs, and wonders confirm with signs the preaching of God's Word.**

And they went out and preached everywhere, the Lord working with them and confirming the word through the accompanying signs. (Mark 16:20)

Miracles, signs, and wonders give credibility. They penetrate the intellectual and humanistic minds that are opposed the gospel.

- **Miracles, signs, and wonders are proof that Jesus was raised from the dead and lives forever.**

And with great power the apostles gave witness to the resurrection of the Lord Jesus. And great grace was upon them all. (Acts 4:33)

Miracles done in the name of Jesus are the supernatural evidences of His *resurrection* (178). And, if Jesus was resurrected, He will do greater things than He did while He walked the earth.

Principles of Operating in Miracles

As you know, miracles originate in the spirit realm and manifest in the natural realm. However, you can enter the spirit realm only by faith, not through the human intellect. This fact yields the following principles:

- **To move in the supernatural, we must disconnect ourselves from reason.**

When we speak about miracles, we must keep in mind that they do not exist in the human intellect or imagination, but only in the supernatural dimension, where reason has no access. To perform miracles, we must remove all reason, because very little of what God does makes sense in the natural.

The majority of what Jesus said to His disciples made little sense to them when He said it.

- **Under the anointing, the miracles go hand in hand with faith.**

Miracles don't happen just like that. We have to *operate* (179) by the principle of faith and the anointing. God always moves in His glory by His sovereignty and His initiative. Likewise, we often have to operate by our own initiative in the anointing, the gifts, or by faith.

- **Miracles should be everyday happenings, not isolated events.**

And through the hands of the apostles many signs and wonders were done among the people. (Acts 5:12)

In some churches, miracles take place only when a famous evangelist visits the city. This is not how it should be! Every believer has received a mandate from God, along with His *dynamis* power and *exusia* authority, to heal the sick, perform miracles, and cast out demons. This is Jesus manifesting His life through us!

- **Miracles should be declared the _instant_ (180) they manifest.**

By faith we understand that the worlds were framed by the word of God.

(Hebrews 11:3)

In Greek, the verb *frame* means "to render...to fit, sound, complete...to mend (what has been broken or rent), to repair...equip, put in order, arrange, adjust." Therefore, according to this verse, our faith tells us that the universe was rendered, fit, completed, mended, repaired, equipped, ordered, arranged, and adjusted by the Word of God. Major manifestations of God's supernatural power are evident today, but the only ones that remain are those which are declared and confirmed. Some people receive miracles but never testify of it. This causes them to lose their miracles a short time later. When a miracle is not declared, its presence in the natural realm becomes illegal. Healing and the miracle of deliverance will not remain unless we testify to them.

Miracles must be received and declared; otherwise, they will not stay.

The condition for a miracle to remain is to _verbally_ (181) declare it. I once asked God why so few miracles take place among His people if His presence is so strong and belongs to everyone. God's answer was that miracles are always taking place, but people fail to declare and testify to them. Therefore, we must testify and declare our miracle!

- **We were educated to adapt to the natural reality and not to miracles.**

Our reality is determined by the natural dimension. If something miraculous happens, it is hard to understand because it is seen as an isolated event. This has to change. We must reach the point of total persuasion and conviction that God is supernatural and that He continues to perform miracles. This has nothing to do with "talking up" God but rather seeing and acknowledging His manifested presence. If God cannot heal the sick or perform miracles, then we must stop calling Him God. If the supernatural offends people, it is because they don't know Him. God cannot be defined without acknowledging the supernatural within Him.

Men criticize everything they cannot produce.

- **Miracles exist in the *now*, not in time.**

Jesus never prayed for a sick person, but He did declare the Word in the present, with power and authority. He would say, "Be healed," or "Be free," because He realized that the kingdom of God had already come. Jesus essentially said, "Your miracle is now!" He continually broke the laws of time, space, and matter.

Some preachers prophesy miracles for the _future_ (182). As a result, their people seek healing only and not miracles. Other pastors have caused miracles to be delayed because they speak of them only in the future tense, saying, "God *will* create a miracle," or "God *will* bring a revival," or "God *will* visit us with His glory." Rarely do they declare what God is doing and saying *now*.

Faith is for now! This is the principle required to receive your miracle.

Most of the men and women who received or performed a miracle in the Bible broke the laws of time, for instance:

• The Syro-Phoenician woman

Then Jesus answered and said to her, "O woman, great is your faith! Let it be to you as you desire." And her daughter was healed from that very hour.   (Matthew 15:28)

Jesus had told this woman that it was not her time because He had not yet died or been resurrected. So, how did she receive her healing? I believe it is because Jesus entered the spirit realm by faith, went to the foundation of the world, and brought her daughter's healing into the now.

• Lazarus

[Martha] said to [Jesus], "Yes, Lord, I believe that You are the Christ, the Son of God, who is to come into the world."…Jesus said to her, "Did I not say to you that if you would believe you would see the glory of God?"   (John 11:27, 40)

Jesus lived in the power of God in *the ＿＿now＿＿*[183]; Martha spoke only of His future resurrection. Jesus had to surpass her intellect and reason in order to lead her into eternity, where everything is in the *now*, the eternal present. That is where Jesus went to get Lazarus and bring him into a new life.

Most believers have a future mentality, not a now mentality.

Who Can Operate in the Flow of Miracles?

• Believers who change their mentality by revelation and the wisdom of the Holy Spirit

That the God of our Lord Jesus Christ, the Father of glory, may give to you the spirit of wisdom and revelation in the knowledge of Him.   (Ephesians 1:17)

God gives us revelation when we have renewed our minds according to His thoughts. Then, He gives us the concepts, such as "how." When the Spirit of wisdom and revelation is absent, it is replaced by "common ＿＿information＿＿ [184]." Each revelation given by God includes the way or method to carry it out because the Spirit of wisdom is in it. We cannot do anything if God does not tell us how to do it. If we don't know the "how," how will we do it?

• Believers who believe

And these signs will follow those who believe.   (Mark 16:17)

Note that this passage says that the signs *"will follow those who believe."* It does not say that they "will follow only the preacher or pastor." It seems that very few of the signs noted in Mark 16 follow today's believers, mostly due to unbelief.

"Go into all the world and preach the gospel to every creature" (verse 15). The Greek word for *"go"* is *poreu,* meaning "to lead over, carry over, transfer…to pursue the journey on which one has entered, to continue on one's journey." We will never be used to perform miracles with God's supernatural power if we don't dare to go, or journey, and gather the harvest.

To *"go"* implies continuous action. In other words, everywhere we go, whether on an airplane or a bus, we should be about our mission of healing the sick. The Greek word derives from another word that means "beyond, on the other side." This implies a penetration or piercing.

• Believers who become a sign

Here am I and the children whom the LORD has given me! We are for signs and wonders in Israel from the LORD of hosts. (Isaiah 8:18)

When we seek Jesus, not only will signs follow us, but we will also *become a sign* [185]. This is conditional, however, because signs will follow us only if we go. If we remain rooted, nothing will follow us. We are the living, genuine testimony of the wonderful work of Jesus Christ in our lives, through which He saved us, transformed us, forgave us, and made us to become a sign for the whole world to see.

• Believers who move in supernatural boldness

Grant to Your servants that with all boldness they may speak Your word. (Acts 4:29)

Jesus is as much the miracle-maker today as He was when He walked the earth. Humanity needs a touch of His miraculous power as never before. Wherever a man of God demonstrates his supernatural boldness and faith in God's Word, healing, miracles, signs, and wonders will take place, and people will be drawn to Christ.

Every believer can move in miracles, signs, and wonders, because they are available to everyone who preaches the gospel—the revelation that Jesus lives and will manifest Himself through us when we surrender our pride and humble ourselves. He wants to use our humanity so that we can become channels of blessings through signs and wonders.

If you need a miracle of healing, I want to pray for you now, declaring that while you read this book, you will be healed:

Father, in the name of Jesus, I order every person who is sick or needs a creative miracle in his or her body—a new organ or physical healing—to be healed at this moment. I order every person to be healed, delivered, and transformed right now! Furthermore, I ask for those who are skeptics and need a visible sign of Your supernatural power to receive a miracle. I further declare that everything covered in this book will manifest in visible and tangible ways in their lives. Perform a miracle, manifest Your signs, and show them a wonder as they read, so they will believe that Jesus is the Son of God, that He lives, and that He loves them. Amen.

9

Principles, Concepts, and Revelations for Operating in the Supernatural

This chapter is the result of having seen God perform all kinds of healings, deliverances, transformations, salvations, miracles, signs, and wonders. Here you will learn the concepts, principles, and fundamentals that will make you desire more of His power until your passion leads you to experience the supernatural power of God in your life.

1. It is crucial to maintain a personal prayer life that perseveres continually.

Now it came to pass, as He was praying in a certain place, when He ceased, that one of His disciples said to Him, "Lord, teach us to pray." (Luke 11:1)

Jesus was praying with His disciples, but only one, *Peter* [186], asked Him to teach them to pray. Perhaps Peter asked this because he understood that all of the healings and other miraculous works of Jesus were made possible by His prayer life. Indeed, Jesus' continuous and persistent prayer life was the main force behind all the miracles, signs, and wonders He performed. Furthermore, prayer directly connected Jesus to the power and authority to deliver the oppressed by casting out their demons.

Hours spent with God turn into minutes spent with men.

Jesus' Prayer Life...

- opened the heavens.
- caused God's power to be manifested everywhere He went.
- helped Him to *choose* [187] His disciples.
- filled Him with the power to heal the masses and deliver them from demons.
- caused God's power to permeate His body and clothing, with the result being that people were healed by His mere touch.
- produced authority and the anointing for the disciples to heal the sick. They did not carry the message of the kingdom under their own anointing but under the anointing produced by the prayer life of Jesus.
- revealed Jesus' true identity to the disciples.
- awakened within His disciples a deep desire to pray.

- taught the disciples the need and the power of persisting in prayer.
- produced zeal for God's house.
- kept Peter's faith from failing in the midst of a trial.
- led Jesus to fight and win the war against _death_ [188]. Thanks to His life of prayer, He obtained the resurrection even before going to the cross.

Jesus' prayer life, and His intimate relationship with the Father, produced a supernatural atmosphere to loosen miracles and cast out demons everywhere He went.

2. Corporate prayer and intercession are just as important as personal prayer.

Another necessity of operating in the supernatural is the atmosphere produced by corporate prayer and worship, as well as the intercession of a church or community that loosens God's presence to perform miracles and healing.

God has blessed me with a wife who has a strong calling for prayer and intercession. Over a period of about fourteen years, she fully developed a ministry of intercession in our church. She begins each day at three in the morning and prays until seven, alongside an army of intercessors who accompany her without apprehension. Personal and corporate prayer are the keys that have created the supernatural atmosphere that rests upon our ministry. Today, we have intercessors and musicians who pray, praise, and worship God together with the people twenty-four hours a day. This _edifies_ [189] God's throne and produces supernatural manifestations that demonstrate His power and glory.

3. It is necessary to have revelation, or revealed knowledge, and God's wisdom.

That the God of our Lord Jesus Christ, the Father of glory, may give to you the spirit of wisdom and revelation in the knowledge of Him. (Ephesians 1:17)

In the Spirit realm, we must learn to flow with the channels of spiritual access because natural channels are inoperable there. To what was Paul referring when he spoke of *"the spirit of wisdom and revelation in the knowledge of Him"*? He was referring to the fact that the spirits of wisdom and revelation teach us how to flow in the supernatural. Many miracles remain unused in eternity because they cannot manifest until their "how" is known. To enter into the supernatural, it takes more than confessing and declaring, more than believing or personal effort. There is no access without revelation.

Without revelation, there is no access to the supernatural.
If we don't have access, it is because we don't have faith to possess it.

Many revivals in this country and throughout the world have died due to a lack of continuous revelation of what was to come. This lack will cause people to become stagnant. After a time, the revival turns into _maintenance_ [190] services where nothing new ever happens. Eventually, this happens in almost every revival because the revelation of the Holy Spirit stops.

When you receive an impartation without revelation,
it cannot remain in your spirit.

How Does the Spirit of Wisdom Work?

Most Christians will say that they believe in miracles. So, why can't they flow in them? It is because they lack revelation, which, combined with the spirit of wisdom, gives access to the supernatural.

Dr. Oral Roberts, who laid hands on more than one million people, shared with me one of his revelations. He said that whenever he was about to minister, he would lock himself in his room beforehand to pray and seek the face of God. He would not leave until he could feel God's power in his right hand. Only then did he know that he was ready for the sick to be healed. According to this principle, his hand had been anointed to heal the sick. That was the *how* God had shown him. Of course, it will not always happen the same way, but it does begin to help us to understand that there is a *how* that God's revelation will give us.

If there is an absence of revealed knowledge, or revelation, there will be no impartation or progress of faith.

For each revelation God gives, He will work something *new* [191]. This is why it is so important for people to learn the *how*. There are few principles of the spirit realm operating in the church today because of a lack of revelation and an absence of the spirit of wisdom.

On the other hand, the world has its own principles, and it knows *how* to behave within the natural realm. The world collects information, performs experiments, uses trial and error, and develops concepts and practices that can be transferred to future generations through education and practical application.

No leader can take you where he has never been or beyond his knowledge.

The Son can do nothing of Himself, but what He sees the Father do; for whatever He does, the Son also does in like manner.   (John 5:19)

You cannot have faith to do that which you don't know how to do.

As it has now been revealed by the Spirit to His holy apostles and prophets....
                                                        (Ephesians 3:5)

***Apostles and prophets bring revelation.
Without them, the church is limited to basic doctrine.***

In most cases, whatever a particular church knows today is due to the ministries of the pastor, evangelist, and teacher exclusively. The result is that the fundamental doctrine of Christianity is *limited* [192], because these offices often do not include such important aspects as apostolic revelation—revelation for *now*. Apostolic revelation breaks new ground by declaring what the Father is saying and doing at this moment in time. This causes the heavens to loosen what God has authorized for earth. When the Holy Spirit reveals something through the apostles and prophets, heaven can no longer contain it. It must be released!

4. Thanksgiving, praise, and worship to God are vital.

But You are holy, enthroned in the praises of Israel. (Psalm 22:3)

Another essential practice to flow in the supernatural is praise, which is the translation from the Hebrew word *tehillah*, which means "a praise, song or hymn of praise...adoration, thanksgiving (paid to God)." It is a joyful hymn that praises the powerful deeds of our Lord. Another word in that verse is *"enthroned,"* which is the Hebrew word *yashab*, meaning "to dwell, remain, sit, abide...to cause to sit." This makes it clear that God wants more than to just pay us a visit. He wants to stay, to get comfortable, and to govern His people who rejoice in His victories. And yet, this can occur only after thanksgiving, praise, and worship. Only when we build a throne with these three elements will God manifest among us.

In thanksgiving, we recognize His goodness; in praise, we recognize His *greatness* [193] and amazing works; and, in worship, we recognize His majesty, sovereignty, and glory.

What Is Thanksgiving?

Enter into His gates with thanksgiving, and into His courts with praise. Be thankful to Him, and bless His name. (Psalm 100:4)

Gratitude and thanksgiving are the keys to loosening God's supernatural power because they build a place—a throne—where God can dwell among us.

What Is Praise?

Praise is the proclamation and declaration of God's powerful deeds, which are articulated with jubilee, excitement, loud sounds, music, applause, shouts, and dance. To praise is to exalt God in a brilliant, extravagant celebration with powerful sounds that border on the ridiculous. It also makes us look like people who have lost their heads and their good sense. Biblically speaking, praise is a *celebration* [194] that breaks all barriers, making it able to *penetrate* [195] a hostile environment.

If we want to experience deep worship, we need vibrant praise.
It is the only way to see God's glory manifest.

What Is Worship?

In the Old Testament, *worship* is the Hebrew word *shachah*, which means "to bow down, prostrate oneself...before superior in homage...before God." It is an act of reverence and humiliation. In the New Testament, it is the Greek word *proskyneo*, which comes from the words *pros*, meaning "to the advantage of," and *kyon*, meaning "to kiss, like a dog licking his master's feet." With this in mind, worship, or *proskyneo*, is bowing down in respect and reverence and kissing the hands and feet of a superior. It is the ultimate expression of submission and reverence for the purpose of humbly begging someone to do something. It is comparable to a dog licking its master's hand as a demonstration of its affection.

Then she came and worshipped Him, saying, "Lord, help me!" (Matthew 15:25)

Worship, then, is a humble, respectful attitude and *reverence* [196] to God demonstrated by physical acts expressed through unselfish and sacrificial service.

Praise recognizes God's powerful works, while worship acknowledges the person of God.

Both the Old and New testaments describe the posture of the body when praising and worshipping. It has nothing to do with what we say but with the attitude in which we say it. Praise and worship go beyond physical posture. They are an attitude of the spirit, body, and soul. Once we have thanked, praised, and worshipped God, His glory will descend. His presence is the sign of His habitation, and that the throne upon which He sits has been edified.

Then Abram fell on his face, and God talked with him. (Genesis 17:3)

How Much Time Should We Devote to Worship?

Praise until the spirit of worship descends; worship until His glory manifests.

What keeps God's presence from manifesting? It is our lack of sufficient worship. It is because we fail to build His throne with our meaningless singing and our incorrect attitudes. On the other hand, when we build God's throne with our worship, Satan cannot remain near us.

Let us look at a series of concepts concerning praise and worship and how to connect with the flow of the supernatural.

- **Praise and worship cause God to** *manifest* [197].

And one cried to another and said: "Holy, holy, holy is the LORD of hosts; the whole earth is full of His glory!" And the posts of the door were shaken by the voice of him who cried out, and the house was filled with smoke. (Isaiah 6:3–4)

When we praise wholeheartedly, we incite God to reveal Himself, as He did in Scripture. In the verse above, when God was worshipped, He revealed His glory. Worship loosens the seals of revelation. When worship does not reach God's throne, revelation cannot take place. Also, when the amount of worship is lacking, the prophetic will be limited in the revelation they receive, and, as a result, creative miracles will not take place. One reason the Bible compares the Word to a hammer (see Jeremiah 23:29) is because, in some places, the atmosphere is so hard to break through that it must be hammered away. But this occurs only when there is insufficient or ineffective worship.

- **Worship in spirit and in truth takes place when we are no longer aware of ourselves but only of God.**

God is Spirit, and those who worship Him must worship in spirit and truth.

(John 4:24)

Worship is a _mandate_ [198]. It has nothing to do with how we feel. Genuine worship is complete when we forget ourselves and focus only on God. We are not worshipping God when we are thinking about ourselves and our circumstances. If we are continually worried about what other people think of us, we are not worshipping. If we continue to occupy our minds with the concerns of our day, we are not worshipping.

- **Worship reveals where God is: a place called *there*.**

Surely the Lord is in this place, and I did not know it.   (Genesis 28:16)

If we want to know where God is, we must worship Him *there*—wherever we are. The Word says, *"Where two or three are gathered together in My name, I am **there***" (Matthew 18:20, emphasis added).

Jacob also found such a place. The desert was the *there* where God met with His people. (See Genesis 28:10–16.) In Adam's case, the Garden of Eden was *there*. (See Genesis 2.) The Lord makes a _divine_ [199] appointment with us and names the place. When we find that place—our *there*—through worship, we will see what He is doing and hear what He is saying.

There is the place where you meet with God through worship.

- **The level of praise and worship determines the type of miracles that will take place in a service.**

If the praise and worship you offer are not enough, someone with a headache may receive healing, but not someone with terminal cancer. Although there are services in which the level of praise and worship is greater than others, we must always strive to raise our level if we want to see His glory.

Also, when we praise and worship God but our lifestyle is not holy, we will not be able to ascend into His presence because we are weighted down. Anything that is not aligned with God will be a weight keeping us from rising to higher levels of worship. The Bible calls this weight *sin*.

Let us lay aside every weight, and the sin which so easily ensnares us.

(Hebrews 12:1)

No church service should regress to a previous, lower level of worship. If the worship in each service does not reach higher than the last, there is no ascension.

Some people are more aware of their own circumstances than they are of Jesus.

- **The main reason we worship is to seek _intimacy_ [200] for the purpose of producing life.**

If our worship cannot produce life, it is dead. Worship is an intimate relationship, much like that between a husband and wife. Worship, too, is planned and intentional. But if our worship is based on God's love, why do we need to be told to sing and raise our hands?

Too much of what takes place during worship in the church today has to do with the soul. It is a worship that produces emotions but too often fails to touch the spirit. Too many of the songs we sing—be they traditional, cultural, or contemporary—center on our earthly needs. When the needs of the earthly realm become our god, our worship becomes idolatry. Worship should reveal God's existence, not satisfy our own flesh. This type of impotent worship is based on our selfish human attitudes.

Our worship will always be *linked* [201] to the revelation we have of God. We cannot praise someone we don't know. We can worship only what we know. The more intimate our knowledge of God, the more details we will have to acknowledge Him and His worth. For this reason, some believers are incapable of praising and worshipping God for long periods of time. They run out of words and stamina because they don't know whom they are worshipping.

- **Praise and worship release the atmosphere of glory and God's presence.**

If we are worshippers in spirit and in truth, we will edify His throne and build a dwelling place that God can inhabit among our new songs. This type of worship will heal the sick, create miracles, transform lives, and glorify God, thereby producing new life in each person at our services.

5. We must build a spiritual atmosphere.

God has always spoken from the cloud of His glory. Thus, it is important that we know how to build a spiritual atmosphere.

What Is Atmosphere?

In science, atmosphere is the layer of gases surrounding a planet. Spiritually speaking, it is the area that surrounds the believer. Spiritual atmosphere is the cloud of God's *presence* [202] that surrounds us. On cold days, if you go outside, you can see your breath when you exhale. In other words, you can see the atmosphere produced by your breath. Praise and worship produce the breath of God in our midst—and His breath gives life.

We must create a celestial atmosphere for miracles, healing, and wonders to take place, an ambiance where we are able to see the words we speak. Sometimes, people will fixate on things in which faith cannot operate. If this happens, change the atmosphere or ambiance.

When Jesus left Nazareth, it was not to prove a theological point or to demonstrate that He was the Son of God. Jesus left because the atmosphere was wrong. (See Mark 6:5–6.) Many people are dying in places where the *supernatural* [203] is nonexistent, where neither the life nor the presence of God can be experienced because a divine atmosphere was never generated. Prayer and intercession are not practiced, and the praise and worship are insufficient to build the tabernacle where God's glory can manifest.

Worship establishes the divine atmosphere on earth.

From God's perspective, everything that is stuck on earth is due to the fall of man. In the beginning, heaven and earth were as one, but, when man sinned, a separation took place—a dislodging. The glory of God no longer manifested in the natural realm. The only way to bring it back is through praise and worship. Understanding this leads us to the realization that we cannot rush praise or worship during services. The duration of praise and worship depends on the place. If the atmosphere is hard to pierce, it will take longer to build the throne. Where the atmosphere already exists, one can go directly into worship.

Three Important Revelations Concerning the Spiritual Atmosphere:

- We must _perceive_ [204] or discern the atmosphere in any given place.
- We must _loosen_ [205] and declare what we perceive in the atmosphere.
- We must _take_ [206] and receive what is loosened in that atmosphere.

6. Know the law of response.

Many Christians have seen excesses and abuses committed by those claiming to walk in the supernatural and have therefore rejected it completely. We must learn to respond to supernatural power without fear and skepticism. Sometimes, Christians try to seek neutral ground on which they can continue to believe in God without having to risk taking a step of faith. They fail to see that this makes them useless to God and unable to bless other people. Furthermore, this type of Christian represents no threat to the enemy. Today, some preachers work hard to induce their people to respond to what God is doing. Still others have no idea how to do this, or even that they should do it. Some religious folks resist the miraculous because they think it has to do with the emotions exclusively.

We cannot stand rigidly by, doing nothing. We must praise and worship God. He wants to be celebrated, not tolerated. God must be loved, His glory yearned for, and His power perceived.

We will be judged for our lack of response when we are in God's presence and power.

How Does the Law of Response Operate?

And the power of the Lord was present to heal them.   (Luke 5:17)

In Luke 5, a multitude of people had gathered and were ready *"to be healed by Him of their infirmities"* (verse 15). In other words, the atmosphere was _ready_ [207] to produce miracles. Still, nothing happened. Perhaps they were waiting for Jesus to lay hands on them or to call them by name. Someone had to take hold of the supernatural. Soon, an individual who arrived late made his way in and, by force, took his miracle from the supernatural atmosphere that had been created by Jesus' prayer life. This bedridden man was lowered down to Jesus from a hole in the roof of the house! Luke wrote that *"the power of the Lord was present to heal them."* The power of God meets every need, and His grace encompasses all things—healing, deliverance, and so forth. It is necessary, however, that we respond like the man in Luke 5, or God's power will depart.

The realm of God's power that does not find a response does not remain.

In some churches, there are believers who used to know how to respond to God's power but then became too religious. They used to freely yell and dance during worship, but now they think of themselves as being too dignified for that kind of thing. This is partly why God allows (rather than causes) pain in our lives. When it hurts, we have no choice but to cry out, forgetting our reputation, and praise Him wholeheartedly. Many people who have suffered much praise God continuously.

God's power is present; it only waits for us to respond, regardless of what we need. Those who have faith to act, do it now!

God loves spontaneity. Anything else is just a mechanical, empty response. Feel free to praise, worship, dance, shout, and respond in ways that you have never responded before. Remember, we are *responding* (208) to God's anointing and glory.

7. Understand the law of expectation.

So he gave them his attention, expecting to receive something from them. (Acts 3:5)

Faith manifests what was already predetermined; therefore, there is expectancy for something to happen.

When people visit our church for the first time, they typically have not experienced the supernatural and do not come with the faith to believe for a miracle. I cannot lay hands on people who do not expect anything to happen. In some cases, they become offended at this, but no one can give them what they are not ready to receive. As believers, we must always expect to receive a miracle, healing, deliverance, or some other supernatural event.

God is loosening a supernatural expectancy in all believers. When He does, regardless of who is preaching, people will be able to come and take their miracle from the eternal realm.

8. Declare the Word with conviction that the words you speak will come to pass.

We cannot declare the Word of God without having *foreknowledge* (209) of what will happen. If we don't want something to happen, we shouldn't declare anything. If we are going to speak to a blind person but don't expect his sight to return, we shouldn't say anything. If we tell the lame to stand up but we have no expectation that anything will happen, we shouldn't speak. If we speak to a deaf-mute and fully expect that he will hear and speak, then we must speak, declare, and wait for him to hear and speak. There should be no doubt in our minds that the words we speak will do what they were sent to do. If we have the smallest doubt about something happening, we have not yet overcome the limitations of our faith. We are still in bondage to time, matter, and space. We cannot speak to matter until we have control and dominion over it. Do we now understand why intellectual knowledge is worthless when it comes to spiritual matters? To move in the supernatural, we must go beyond the natural, material realm. We must begin to exercise dominion over the laws of nature.

Don't speak the Word if you doubt that anything will happen.

By the word of the LORD the heavens were made, and all the host of them by the breath of His mouth. (Psalm 33:6)

When God's Word is spoken and it joins with the breath of the Holy Spirit, it produces an explosion called "_Creative power_ (210)" and is confirmed by the Holy Spirit. This divine, supernatural power will make the blind see, the deaf hear, the mute speak, and the lame walk—God still performs creative miracles. If we speak like God, with the intent to see something happen, there is no alternative: something will happen. It can be declared without any margin of error.

...upholding all things by the word of His power. (Hebrews 1:3)

Confession _is speaking what God has said;_ rhema _is speaking what God is saying now._

In conclusion, we have learned many principles and concepts related to flowing in supernatural, including prayer, intercession, revelation, praise, worship, atmosphere, the laws of reaction and expectancy, and speaking the creative Word. All of these things work together to enable God's glory to manifest in order to heal the sick, deliver the captives, and proclaim the gospel of Jesus throughout the earth so that His name may be glorified. This is how the world will know and be able to experience our supernatural God.

10

Jesus Manifesting His Supernatural Power through the Believer

The book of Acts marks the end of Jesus' ministry and the beginning of the ministry of His church. We were birthed to continue doing what He began. This is why He empowered us with the same power and authority He had received from the Father, so that everyone who believes in that power can access it and do the same works as Jesus. The book of Acts records the many miraculous works performed by the apostles as they were led by the Holy Spirit, but it also opens the way for every believer to participate in the personal victories God gives to him as he obeys in the name of Jesus.

An *act* refers to _actions_ [211], works, or events. It is something we do, such as preaching the Word with demonstrations of God's supernatural power to heal and perform miracles. It also incorporates the progress of the fulfillment of the Great Commission. In the same way, you and I should be able to write a similar account of the works of the Holy Spirit performed through our lives. The first apostles seemed to be working constantly. They healed the sick, rebuked demons, and performed miracles. They shouldered the responsibility of advancing the kingdom of God. They formed the first church. Believe it or not, Jesus mentioned the church considerably less than He did the kingdom.

What Names Are Given to the Church in Scripture?

In the Bible, God's people are referred to by different names: church, body, work, temple, family, _bride_ [212], and army. Some say the church is like a hospital, but the Bible never refers to it with this term. Yes, the church restores and heals the sick, the fallen, the sad, and the depressed, but this is not its most important function.

What Is the Church?

The church is the body of Christ. The Greek word for "church" is *ekklesia*, which means "a gathering of citizens called out from their homes into some public place...for the purpose of deliberating." The origin of this word is found in two Hebrew terms: *edah*, meaning "divine testimonies," and *qahal*, meaning "to assemble, gather...for religious reasons." *Ekklesia* has two characteristics: first, there is a *calling* of individuals to gather together; second, there is a *purpose* for the calling. In short, *ekklesia* is a group of people called to gather for a specific purpose. For the church, we are called by Jesus for the purpose of carrying out His will on earth.

In other words, we were called out of the world to form the body of Christ and to obey Jesus, its Head. However, the Head can do nothing unless the *body* (213) is willing to move. If my head wants to go through a doorway, it makes the decision, and the body must obey and move. If I want to pick up something from the floor, the head will decide before the hand stretches to perform the corresponding action. Likewise, Jesus—as the Head—has plans, desires, a purpose, a mission, and a mandate, but these cannot be carried out unless the body obeys. In my case, even if my head wanted to leave my body behind and carry out the plan on its own, it can't because the function of the head is to command, and the function of the body is to execute, or carry out, that command.

When God tells us to do something, it is because He is not going to do it for us.

For example, God told us to *proclaim* (214) the gospel of the kingdom throughout the world, beginning in our homes, neighborhoods, cities, and nations, but He also told us to make disciples, heal the sick, and cast out demons. If we would obey, He promised that signs would follow. (See Mark 16:20.)

> *And I also say to you that you are Peter, and on this rock I will build My church, and the gates of Hades shall not prevail against it.* (Matthew 16:18)

Jesus did not delegate the task of building of His church to anyone. He did it Himself, founded on the revelation, or revealed knowledge, that He was the Messiah, the Lord of Lords and King of Kings.

Ekklesia was also used to designate the state governmental body, which was led by its male citizens. For Christians, the church comprises people around the world who are called to establish a kingdom government and authority on earth by proclaiming the gospel of Jesus Christ with signs and miracles. Unfortunately, today, there is insufficient evidence of God's kingdom government on earth because we have failed to fully exercise our responsibility as administrators of His government.

As the church, we are even *responsible* (215) for many bad things taking place because we have not used our delegated authority to declare them illegal. If we want to change the nation, we must begin by changing the church. Are we aware of our responsibilities? In Rome, once a law was passed, it could not be challenged. Local officials, however, could issue decrees over the areas they ruled. Similarly, Jesus created our laws, and they cannot be challenged. But we can make decrees.

> *Whatever you bind (declare to be improper and unlawful) on earth must be what is already bound in heaven; and whatever you loose (declare lawful) on earth must be what is already loosed in heaven.* (Matthew 16:19 AMP)

If it is done in heaven, why can't it be done on earth? We must learn to speak new decrees in order to make the laws of the kingdom come to *pass* (216) on earth. Jesus carries out His eternal goals through the church, regardless of how long it takes. In fact, it has taken twenty centuries to carry the gospel to the nations, and we still have not finished reaching the last corners of the earth. We must flood the nations with miracles, signs, and wonders. Jesus will not do the job that we were entrusted with. Many believers lack supernatural authority because they have not learned to walk under supernatural authority. Some are rebellious and must learn to submit to the Head: Jesus.

Anything not subject to the Head is not the body or the church.

What Are the Goals of the Church?

1. To proclaim the gospel of the kingdom throughout the world

And this gospel of the kingdom will be preached in all the world as a witness to all the nations, and then the end will come. (Matthew 24:14)

Believers are supposed to be the *salt* [217] of the earth and light of the world (see Matthew 5:13–14), ambassadors, fishers of men, armor bearers, witnesses, kings, priests, representatives of Jesus, and peacemakers. In essence, we are to be "little Christs."

2. To make disciples of all nations

Go therefore and make disciples of all the nations. (Matthew 28:19)

In our church, we have thousands of disciples, both in the United States and throughout twenty-five other nations. Each disciple is being trained and equipped to heal the sick, preach the gospel of the kingdom, and perform miracles, signs, and wonders in his neighborhood, territory, and city of the world.

3. To manifest the life of the *kingdom* [218]

That the life of Jesus also may be manifested in our mortal flesh. (2 Corinthians 4:11)

The life of the kingdom is the resurrected life of Jesus, which has been made available, by faith, to every believer. The life of Jesus is made manifest in our mortal bodies. It is what I call "divine health and healing." If we have it, then we can also minister that life of resurrection to others to heal and deliver them.

Unless a grain of wheat falls into the ground and dies, it remains alone; but if it dies, it produces much grain. (John 12:24)

Before Jesus went to the cross, He gave His disciples a kingdom principle that would guarantee their success and manifest the life of God: If you plant a seed, it will die; however, when the seed dies, it will *reproduce* [219] a hundred times over. The plant that grows out of the dead seed will be the same as the seed because it has the seed's DNA. Until that moment, Jesus had been unable to reproduce His life in the lives of His disciples. To do that, He had to go to the cross to die for the sins of humanity and to redeem us. His sacrifice also made available the seed that, when planted in the spiritual womb of a believer, could reproduce its exact genetic components. Because of that seed, we can reach the measure of the perfect Man—Jesus.

4. To manifest the authority and power of the kingdom

Behold, I give you the authority to trample on serpents and scorpions, and over all the power of the enemy, and nothing shall by any means hurt you. (Luke 10:19)

God gave us His power when He sent His Holy Spirit the day we recognized Jesus as the Lord of our lives. God gave us His authority when He paid the wages of our sins at the cross. At that moment, Jesus made us coheirs with Him. In other words, the day we were born again, we also became God's children with the authority, power, and legal right to exercise divine power in order to manifest the kingdom and carry out the mission Jesus commanded us to do.

5. To expand the kingdom of God

At the onset of creation, God created man to govern and exercise dominion and lordship over the earth. We—the believers—are the only _instruments_ [220] God uses to carry out His will and to expand His dominion upon the face of the earth, which we accomplish by proclaiming and demonstrating God's kingdom.

6. To proclaim the kingdom *without* visible demonstrations

John performed no sign, but all the things that John spoke about this Man were true.
(John 10:41)

John the Baptist preached about the coming of Jesus, but he was not able to manifest any miraculous signs of the kingdom. Likewise, today, some men and women preach the truth and have the right doctrine but also are unable to demonstrate the supernatural power of God with miracles and signs because teaching, proclaiming, and announcing the kingdom through words alone is only the first phase.

7. To preach the kingdom *with* visible _demonstrations_ [221] of power

But if I cast out demons by the Spirit of God, surely the kingdom of God has come upon you. (Matthew 12:28)

When John the Baptist ended his ministry of announcing God's kingdom, a new phase began: the preaching phase. Jesus began this phase by preaching, teaching, and demonstrating the kingdom with miracles, signs and wonders, and by casting out demons. This was a new, unique occurrence.

The casting out of demons is a visible sign that the kingdom has arrived.

---

8. To advance the kingdom of God by force

And from the days of John the Baptist until now the kingdom of heaven suffers violence, and the violent take it by force. (Matthew 11:12)

A more literal translation of this verse would read, "From the days of John the Baptist until now, the kingdom of God has been governed by force, and only those with power control it." This is the violent phase of our spiritual war—the conflict between the kingdom of God and the kingdom of darkness. In this phase, we preach and teach, establishing and extending God's divine government over new _territories_ [222].

The Church Cooperates with God in the Expansion of the Kingdom

For we are God's fellow workers. (1 Corinthians 3:9)

What Channel Does Jesus Use to Operate on Earth?

Our physical *bodies* (223) are the instruments Jesus uses to operate on earth. All of His plans will be carried out by His body, the Church.

As the body of Christ, we are the only ones capable of putting limits on what Jesus can do on earth. God will not do more than what His body asks or allows—not because He can't or doesn't want to but because He has delegated His gospel, authority, and power to His body. Furthermore, since the kingdom is within us, this makes us extremely valuable. What requirement must be fulfilled in order to operate as His body? The requirement of interdependence. Each member of the body needs the others, and yet, not one member is indispensable. The purpose of the body—the church— is to be used by Jesus to manifest in the natural realm of space, time, and matter. He depends on us in order to operate in this dimension. When Jesus came to earth, He Himself needed a body to carry out His Father's will. The same is true today.

We are the extension of Jesus. Through our bodies, He touches the world.

The Relationship Between the Head and the Body of Christ

And the eye cannot say to the hand, "I have no need of you"; nor again the head to the feet, "I have no need of you."   (1 Corinthians 12:21)

Christ is the Head, and, as such, He cannot tell the hands or feet, "I don't need you." What the Head requires of the feet is the *availability* (224) and willingness to carry out its decisions. Regardless of how talented I might be as a Christian, if I am not available and *willing* (225) to submit to the Head, I am worthless for the kingdom. Christ will use His body to destroy the works of Satan: sickness, oppression, and captivity.

For What Divine Reasons Did God Give Us Bodies?

The main reason God gave us bodies was to make us His habitation and to place His glory within us. God does not live in man-made temples. The temple He designed is your body and mine, and that is where He wants to live.

Behold, the tabernacle of God is with men, and He will dwell with them, and they shall be His people. God Himself will be with them and be their God.   (Revelation 21:3)

God will not dwell permanently in a man-made temple.
He will make His habitation in the temple of His doing.

What Type of Dwelling Place Is God Looking For?

You also, as living stones, are being built up a spiritual house, a holy priesthood.
                                                        (1 Peter 2:5)

After many years and scores of money, Solomon's temple was finally completed. It was an amazing structure. It did not last, though, because it was destroyed by the sin of Israel. That was probably when God decided not continue investing in stone and mortar but in the dust of the earth. With the coming of Christ, we became His _temple_ [226]. He could not have worked with more valuable materials, as we were purchased with blood—the blood of His precious Son, Jesus.

Therefore, as believers, we no longer belong to the devil; we belong to God.

How Does Jesus Minister Today?

Christ in you, the hope of glory. (Colossians 1:27)

The revelation of this mystery is that Jesus lives in you and wants to minister through you. He needs us to lend Him our bodies so that He can reach our families and friends.

Preaching the gospel is limited by man's will to obey what God commanded him to do.

Jesus can visit a sick person or a prisoner using our bodies. He will go in us and with us. He cannot do it any other way. Unfortunately, many people use prayer as an excuse not to go. Please, don't misunderstand. Jesus prayed because it is important to do so, but in many cases, He also *went* to pray for them while He was in a human body.

God anointed Jesus of Nazareth with the Holy Spirit and with power, who went about doing good and healing all who were oppressed by the devil, for God was with Him.
(Acts 10:38)

There are two types of prayer that God will never answer: when we ask Him to do what He has already _done_ [227], and when we ask Him to do what we are _supposed_ [228] to do as His Church. How will Jesus do His part? By using our lives. He will work in you, *"for it is God who works in you both to will and to do for His good pleasure"* (Philippians 2:13).

We must pray, but we also must go and do.

God Entrusted His Gospel to You and Me

The glorious gospel of the blessed God...was committed to my trust. (1 Timothy 1:11)

What Must We Do?

Now that God has restored us and revealed His supernatural power, chosen and anointed us to _go_ [229] in His name and made us His representatives, we must go. We must decide to go!

Jesus served the people, spoke what was needed, and ministered His love and compassion. He has not changed. The only difference between then and now is that now, He does it through you and me. How does this happen? The fullness of His power will be loosened if we meet these basic conditions:

• Total commitment

Surrender without _reservation_ (230) and present your body as a living sacrifice so your hands can become His hands, your feet can become His feet, and your mouth can become His mouth. Then, you can heal the sick, deliver the captives, save the lost, perform miracles, signs, and wonders, and manifest His glory everywhere.

• Total obedience

Everyone must decide to obey his Word and keep His mandate. We don't need further _confirmation_ (231); the harvest is ready.

• Total availability

We must be ready the moment the Lord wants to manifest His glory through us.

The only ability God seeks in mankind is availability.

The world is hurting, waiting for a special touch to rescue them from the emptiness of life. To be used by God to bless other people causes incredible joy and is at the heart of Christianity—"*Christ in you, the hope of glory*" (Colossians 1:27), to win souls, proclaim the gospel, and perform miracles, signs, and wonders.

Christ in you, the hope of glory. (Colossians 1:27)

We Were Chosen and Anointed for Action

In Matthew 5–7, Jesus preached His Sermon on the Mount. But when Matthew 8 begins, we see Him perform miracles and demonstrate the things He taught. You would be surprised to see what could happen if you laid hands on the sick, declaring the Word that lives within you.

Can we answer God's call, saying as Isaiah did, *"Here am I! Send Me"* (Isaiah 6:8)? "Lord, I lend You my humanity of my own free will to speak to the lost, encourage the brokenhearted, heal the sick, and deliver the afflicted and those in mourning. Lord, I will serve You. Send me!"

This challenge comes from God to you. Repeat this prayer aloud:

I am a believer—a Christian—and Jesus is my Lord. I believe that Jesus was raised from the dead. He guarantees His promises, and I will experience His supernatural power because Christ is resurrected in me. The Holy Spirit has anointed me with power from above to believe that all things are possible. Jesus is greater than any problem or challenge before me. He lives in me, and the power that raised Him from the dead is working in my life as I speak. Satan knows this and cannot do anything about it. Jesus, You publicly humiliated the enemy and destroyed his works. Now, You live in me, giving me the grace to experience Your power, heal the sick, deliver the captives, perform miracles and marvels in Your name, and preach Your gospel throughout the nations. As long as there is breath within me, Lord, use me wherever I may go to continue Your ministry. Amen.

Answer Key

1. spiritual
2. eternal
3. disclosure
4. suddenly
5. perceiving
6. natural
7. Holy Spirit
8. love
9. wisdom
10. incapable
11. God
12. man
13. origin
14. faith
15. depend
16. time
17. will
18. knowledge
19. revealed
20. natural
21. supernatural
22. time
23. above
24. intervention
25. stand still
26. God
27. Satan
28. alert
29. deceived
30. lordship
31. eyes
32. supernatural
33. understanding
34. dead
35. revelation
36. Ignorance
37. Theology
38. Humanism
39. common sense
40. revealed

41. believed
42. power
43. authority
44. destructive
45. witchcraft
46. reasoning
47. mind
48. charisma
49. limit
50. traditions
51. everything
52. reward
53. honor
54. manifestations
55. vain
56. Doing
57. grieving
58. quenching
59. extinguish
60. advancement
61. willing
62. weak
63. conflict
64. transform
65. Tarry
66. govern
67. Powerful
68. same
69. potential
70. available
71. wrong
72. renewed
73. curse
74. whipped
75. spat
76. refused
77. legs
78. sins
79. iniquity
80. victory

81. Sin
82. priest
83. sacrifice
84. supremacy
85. grace
86. legalistic
87. laws
88. finished
89. forgiven
90. sickness
91. accepted
92. rebellion
93. selfishness
94. cross
95. world
96. permanent
97. preaching
98. extreme
99. fidelity
100. natural
101. dimension
102. eternity
103. senses
104. now
105. problems
106. conviction
107. promised
108. senses
109. influence
110. incapable
111. persuaded
112. Unbelief
113. revelation
114. faith
115. understanding
116. unreasonable
117. judged
118. disconnect
119. stagnant
120. oil

Answer Key

121. anointing
122. olive
123. consecrates
124. measure
125. mantle
126. man
127. intervention
128. spirit
129. bless
130. generation
131. old mantle
132. receive
133. parish
134. criticism
135. familiarity
136. demand
137. inheritance
138. obedience
139. satiated
140. visitation
141. genuinely
142. impart
143. increase
144. glory
145. withdrew
146. disconnected
147. essence
148. visible
149. cloud
150. obeyed
151. creation
152. knowing
153. initiated
154. manifestations
155. works
156. gifts
157. multitudes
158. commanded
159. delegated
160. religion

161. ministry
162. illegal
163. instantaneous
164. progressive
165. demonstration
166. worship
167. prove
168. soul
169. uprooting
170. demonic
171. flexible
172. confirmed
173. validates
174. testify
175. persuade
176. demonstrations
177. evident
178. resurrection
179. operate
180. instant
181. verbally
182. future
183. now
184. information
185. sign
186. Peter
187. choose
188. death
189. edifies
190. maintenance
191. new
192. limited
193. greatness
194. celebration
195. penetrate
196. reverence
197. manifest
198. mandate
199. divine
200. intimacy

201. linked
202. presence
203. supernatural
204. perceive
205. loosen
206. take
207. ready
208. responding
209. foreknowledge
210. creative power
211. actions
212. bride
213. body
214. proclaim
215. responsible
216. pass
217. salt
218. kingdom
219. reproduce
220. instruments
221. demonstrations
222. territories
223. bodies
224. availability
225. willing
226. temple
227. done
228. supposed
229. go
230. reservation
231. confirmation